TEACHER'S MANUAL

WRITING AND ANALYSIS

IN THE LAW

FOURTH EDITION

By

HELENE S. SHAPO
Professor of Law
Director of Legal Writing
Northwestern University School of Law

MARILYN R. WALTER
Professor of Law
Director of the Legal Writing Program
Brooklyn Law School

ELIZABETH FAJANS, Ph.D.
Associate Professor of Legal Writing
Writing Specialist
Brooklyn Law School

———————————

New York, New York

FOUNDATION PRESS

1999

TABLE OF CONTENTS

Appendices

Additional Materials

Chapter One

Introduction to the Legal System and Legal Writing

This chapter introduces students to the American legal system and to the concepts they must master in order to engage in and write legal analysis. If your students take a separate course in legal method or legal analysis, you may want to omit this chapter. Another alternative is to assign the chapter to students to read themselves as an overview, but not spend class time discussing the material. Or you may want to begin about one-third into the chapter with Part III, "The Development of the Law Through the Common Law Process." In this section, we begin to link the analytical material with basic concepts of writing about law in order to show students that they must understand the underlying analytical process in order to write effectively. We have used some examples that pinpoint some common student errors in writing about legal authority.

If your students do not take a basic legal methods course, this chapter is their introduction to our legal system and the sources of legal authority in this country. One of the difficulties law students have in making the transition from writing as an undergraduate to writing in law school is to learn how to use primary authorities of law. These authorities are explained in this and the next two chapters.

After introducing the types of primary authorities, we begin explaining the common law system in detail. We start by explaining how a judicial decision becomes a source of law that binds later judges' decisions. Then, in order to explain which precedents bind a particular court, we explain in Part II the structure of the court systems in terms of the process from trial to appeal, and the parallel systems of state and federal courts. We also indicate in a few places examples of where the two court systems interact. For example, a federal court in a diversity case applies state law.

You may want to add to the top of page nine the topic of when a state court exercises jurisdiction over a federal issue, such as when a state court exercises concurrent jurisdiction over a federally created right of action, or when a defendant in state court raises the issue of whether the application of a state statute is unconstitutional. Most state courts consider that they are bound only by decisions of the Supreme Court of the United States on that issue and employ as persuasive the interpretations of the federal issues decided by lower federal courts, especially the interpretations of those federal courts which have jurisdiction over that state. (One reason is that state decisions are reviewable only by the Supreme Court of the United States.) However, some state courts consider the decisions of lower federal courts as binding. See Richard A. Matasar, Rediscovering "One Constitutional Case": Procedural Rules and the Rejection of the Gibbs Test for Supplemental Jurisdiction, 71 Cal. L. Rev. 1399, 1422 n.94 (1983).

The chapter then explains the nature of a legal system bound by the doctrines of precedent and stare decisis, and the nature of binding and persuasive authority.

In Part III we discuss the meaning of the holding of a case, especially in the context of when a holding is binding. We also discuss this topic in Chapter Two in the discussions of case briefs and of comparing cases. The discussion in Chapter One is more extensive and uses a simple example from a false imprisonment situation. You may consider by-passing this explanation here, perhaps providing a simple explanation that only the actual decision of a case is binding on later courts, and then assign these pages along with the material in Chapter Two. The false imprisonment exercise in Chapter One, Exercise l-B, is developed in Chapter Two.

Even if you postpone assigning the material on holding and dicta until a later chapter, we suggest that you resume with Part IV "Statutes and the Relationship Between Case Law and Statutes." This section introduces students to the importance of enacted law as a primary authority. In this section, we discuss the different types of enacted law, but most of our later discussion about enacted law focuses on statutory law, which is what most first year students are assigned to work with. Chapter Three, for example, is almost entirely about statutory issues.

Part V of this chapter is about citation. This section includes information about plagiarism. The discussion does not explain Bluebook form, but explains the purpose of citation in relation to a system of precedent and the requirements of legal writing.

This part is explained in terms of citation to provide authority for statements, and citation to avoid plagiarism. For example, we note that citation is used in legal writing even for information that is common knowledge in the law, although in undergraduate writing, information that is common knowledge does not require citation. In legal writing, the citation shows authority for the statement; it is not used to avoid plagiarism.

Appendix B contains an explanation of citation form. If you teach citation form in your course, you may want to teach that material next, using Appendix B. We have included a Bluebook exercise assignment at the end of the Appendix.

Exercise 1-A: Answer

This is a simple exercise to distinguish rules, holdings, and dicta. The exercise also makes the point that a rule may come from a private document as well as from enacted law and judicial decisions. The private rule binds only signatories to the document.

      a.   The rule is that the landlord must return the tenant's security deposit within thirty days of the lease's expiration, but may deduct for property damage beyond reasonable wear. The rule comes from the lease.

      b.   Some possibilities for the holding could be "the damage to the carpet [premises] caused by cigarette burns resulted from the tenant's carelessness, not from reasonable wear."

or "Damage to a carpet from cigarette burns is not reasonable wear."

or "The landlord may deduct from the tenant's security deposit for damage caused by cigarette burns because the burns are not reasonable wear."

      c.   Reasonable wear would be frayed spots on the carpet.

Exercise 1-B: Answer

In Chapter Two we include other exercises using the Beta v. Adam facts.

Beta v. Adam. The broadest holding is Answer 1. The descriptions of the parties, of the plaintiff's property, and of the area of confinement are all quite broadly phrased.

Answer 2 is the most narrow. The defendant is described by occupation and relation to the plaintiff, his statement and other activity are included, and the plaintiff's property is identified.

Answer 3 is more like a classroom statement of a holding, but is not as responsive to the particular case. It is written here as a general principle that includes the issue in the case, but does not include any particular facts or the nature of the confinement.

Exercise 1-C: Answer

Answer 1 is the best introduction. It names the statute and sets out its terms, and then concludes about the application of the statutory requirements to the facts of a problem. Answer 2 begins as if the reader knows the statute's requirements and the order in which they are set out.

Exercise 1-D: Answer

1. "The test for determining whether a plaintiff is entitled to attorney's fees involves four factors: whether the litigation provided a public benefit, whether the plaintiff gained financially from the litigation, whether the plaintiff had a personal interest in the materials sought, and whether the government unreasonably withheld the materials. Case cite. The factors usually have equal weight. Case cite. However, if the government acted particularly unreasonably, the last criterion may be more important. Case cite."

The four factors listed in the first sentence of the paragraph most likely come from a case in which all factors are listed. An alternative here is to cite a case after each factor in which just that factor was discussed.

2. The Kent statute permits an unwitnessed will. Statutory cite. This type of will is known as a holographic will. Cite. To be valid, a holographic will must be entirely written and dated by the testator. Statutory cite. The courts have interpreted "dated" to mean month, day, and year. Case cite.

The first citation would be to the probate code of Kent. The second citation would also be to the code unless that term is not used in the code, but the writer has taken that definition from a case or a secondary source, in which case the cite would be to either of those.

Exercise 1-E: Answers

The exercises at the end of the chapter are a wide-ranging exploration of the weight of various kinds of sources with respect to a particular legal problem. These three exercises are very useful in uncovering students' misconceptions and

Chapter Two

Analyzing Legal Authority: Case Law

This chapter is designed to help the students learn how to analyze and synthesize cases. They will be analyzing cases for both the more limited purpose of briefing them for class and the more significant purpose of using precedent to reason how a problem case is likely to be resolved. They will then be introduced to the very important topic of case synthesis, a topic also analyzed in the discussion of small-scale organization in Chapter Five. You may want to delay discussing Part IV until you assign a memorandum or another writing assignment that involves more than one case.

First-year students recognize that cases are a source of legal rules. They can apply these rules and even reach conclusions. But they often fail to understand the importance of the other parts of a case, particularly the facts and the court's reasoning. As a result, their analysis tends to be incomplete. In addition, they have difficulty isolating the holding of a case. Accordingly, this chapter identifies and explains the different parts of a case to help the students better understand each individual case and the way that cases relate to each other. Much of the chapter is focused on reasoning by analogy and applying precedent.

In the discussion of synthesizing cases, three types of synthesis are identified: grouping cases according to the rule they follow, defining the elements of an evolving claim or defense, and identifying factors that courts use to determine how a cause of action can be proven.

Exercise 2-A: Answer

The differences in the facts distinguish the cases, but not in ways that will aid the plaintiff Brown. Some facts favor Brown. For example, he did not walk out of the room. Even if he had the opportunity, he may have been too frightened to attempt to leave. And Brown was in the defendant's office longer than the previous plaintiff. This fact is the strongest for Brown. Five hours is a long time, and it is unusual for an employer to detain someone so long. The other facts tend to prove that Brown stayed voluntarily. The door was not locked so Brown could have left the room, and he had access to a telephone. These two facts make the defendant's case stronger than in the precedent.

Exercise 2-B: Answer

a.   The type of body of water (a river rather than a pond) should not make a difference. The fact of the water being a river alone does not distinguish the cases on grounds of danger. If the river had strong currents or other dangers, then the bodies of water may be distinguished on grounds of hidden danger.

b.   The Paugh decision talks about natural bodies of water; however, the reasoning applies as well to the gravel pit, and the case law on this subject has held that artificial bodies of water are analogous to natural ones. The pit is not dangerous in itself, although it might be more easily fenced or drained.

c.   The lake is a natural body of water and the waterfall is natural. But the waterfall is most likely dangerous because it is a hidden danger not visible from land. The city cannot do much to remedy the situation except put up warning signs.

d.   The abandoned well is also distinguishable. It is dangerous; anyone who falls in would not likely escape; the danger would not be commonly known to children; the well could be enclosed without high cost; and it serves no environmental or recreational purpose.

Exercise 2-C: Answer

Cases dealing with mental capacity to contract often raise interesting questions about the treatment of the elderly and the rights of persons contracting with the mentally ill.

The issue in this case is whether Winter was mentally competent to contract when he signed a contract for the sale of his land. Contracts may be voidable on grounds of mental incompetence if a person, because of his mental illness, was unable to reasonably understand the nature and consequences of the transaction in question.

Facts relevant to whether Winter was mentally incompetent are

a)   facts relevant to the actual sale
    1.   the price which was far below actual value,

Case 3: Statement b. is a more useful formulation of the holding in <u>Beta</u>. The reasoning, which focuses on property of value, can extend to the car.

Exercise 2-G: Answers

a.   The issue in <u>Dale</u> is analogous to the issue in <u>Paugh.</u> In <u>Dale</u>, the issue is whether a hedge with concealed poles surrounding a Hotel is an attractive nuisance so that the Hotel would be liable in negligence to a six-year-old child whose kneecap was injured by a pole hidden in the hedge .

b.   The five elements of attractive nuisance need to be considered in determining whether the facts are analogous or distinguishable.

      For some elements, the facts are analogous. Both the pond in <u>Paugh</u> and the Hotel's hedge in <u>Dale</u> are attractive to young children. In addition, both were places children went and where children could be expected to go. Children, in fact, were constantly trying to get inside the Hotel grounds and being chased away by Hotel guards. Moreover, the children in both of the cases were the same age, six-years-old, and could understand the potential for danger. The children in <u>Paugh</u> had been warned not to go to the pond without their father. The children in <u>Dale</u> could understand the danger of falling from a six-foot hedge, even if they were unaware of the danger of the hidden poles.

      The facts are distinguishable in two ways. The first relates to the question of whether the condition was dangerous in itself. The court in <u>Paugh</u> concluded that the pond was not dangerous in itself, in part because drowning in an ordinary pond was a commonly known danger. The court specifically noted that if there were conditions that caused a particular risk, like a concealed danger, then its decision might be different. In <u>Dale</u>, the risk arose from a concealed danger in a natural condition, the hedge, though poles are not dangerous in themselves as, for example, explosives would be.

      The facts are also distinguishable on whether it was reasonably feasible to prevent access without destroying the condition's utility. The court in <u>Paugh</u> concluded that a fence all around the pond would be prohibitive in cost (though the city was considering draining the pond at a cost of $25,000 in 1979 dollars), and difficult in light of the terrain. It would be easier for the Hotel to erect a fence around the hedge, although the Hotel had earlier decided against making the necessary $20,000 expenditure.

c. The court's reasoning might lead to a different result, because of the difference between a natural condition which has a useful public function (the pond), and a concealed artificial condition (the poles) created only to make trimming the hedge easier and to allow it to grow straighter.

d. The court in Paugh was strongly aware of the state's policy in encouraging the owners of recreational land to make land available to the public. The court was also concerned about the "undue" burden which would be put on landowners to fence off their property. Finally, the court raised a question about whose responsibility it was to care for children – the landowners or the parents. This question was also raised by the Hotel's attorney.

e. Although it is not absolutely clear, an argument could be made in Dale that the holding in Paugh is distinguishable. The poles involved a hidden danger (though not necessarily one that was inherently dangerous) and there is no public policy supporting the public's access to recreational land as there was in Paugh. Moreover, it would be far more feasible for the Hotel to build the fence than for the state and private landowners to fence the numerous bodies of water within the state.

Exercise 2-H: Answer

1. This is a good exercise to assign early in the first semester after the students have become familiar with the principles of precedent and stare decisis. You can either have the students write the answer as if it were the Discussion section in a short memo, beginning with a thesis paragraph, or you could have them omit the thesis paragraph and write the exercise as a case comparison. In any event, it is important to focus the students' attention on the factual similarities and differences between the two cases.

Many students believe that Phil's father was not negligent. A sample response taking the position that Phil's father was not negligent follows. The marginal comments identify the structure of the analysis.

Introductory
"thesis"
paragraph

David Peterson, Sr. is not liable in negligence to Phil Aarons for storing tools in a basement where Peterson's eleven- year-old son was playing with Aarons and where Aarons was injured by the son's attempt to use the tools.

General rule

A person has a duty to protect others against unreasonable risks. Smith v. Allen. One who breaches this duty is negligent and liable for injuries resulting from that negligence. Id.

Legal
conclusion

Peterson did not create an unreasonable risk by storing tools in the basement and should, therefore, not be liable.

Discussion
of
precedent   Topic
              sentence

An adult creates an unreasonable risk of harm by allowing children access to "obviously and intrinsically dangerous" objects. Id. If the child injures another with

Facts and
holding of
precedent

that object, the adult is liable for the resulting injuries. In Smith v. Allen, a father had left a golf club lying in his backyard, and his eleven-year-old son swung the golf club and injured a nine-year-old girl. Id. The court held that the complaint failed to state a claim for negligence on the part of the father because a golf club is not so "obviously and intrinsically dangerous" as to create an

13

unreasonable risk. Unlike a knife, it is not commonly used as a weapon. Id.

Issue # 1
Dangerousness

Aarons might argue that tools like hammers are made of hard metal and are heavy; similarly, nails are metallic and have sharp points. Either could easily hurt someone if left in the hands of a child. However, like the golf club in Smith, the hammer and nails used by David, Jr. are not weapons. Because they are commonly used in a household, they are not so obviously dangerous as to impose a duty upon Peterson, Sr. to protect against unreasonable risks.

Rebuttal to
opposing
argument and
conclusion

Issue # 2
Father's conduct

Even if the tools were dangerous, Peterson created less of a risk than did the Smith defendant. Although Peterson left the tools where he knew his son played, Peterson had stored his tools in a box; he did not leave them out in the open, as the Smith defendant had left his golf club.

Possible
opposing
argument

Although a child is more likely to misuse tools than golf clubs, there is little support in Smith for the position that Peterson, Sr. is negligent because he should have anticipated his son's misuse of the tools. The court

14

Counterargument
and
conclusion

in <u>Smith</u> found insufficient a complaint which alleged that the father "knew or 'should have known' that negligent use of the golf club by children would cause injury to a child." <u>Smith</u>, therefore, implies that if an object is not "obviously and intrinsically dangerous," a defendant cannot be held accountable for a risk that is unlikely to occur.

2. Part 2 of this exercise uses a later case from the same jurisdiction. The students should see that <u>Green</u> does not overrule <u>Smith</u>, but it is highly relevant to the problem and should provide students with additional analysis. Students often pay little attention to a case that may offer relevant ideas, but is not on point. The facts and issue in <u>Green</u> are related to, though not the same as, the facts in <u>Aarons</u>. In <u>Green</u> the object in question was a golf ball, an instrument which the court characterized as a "dangerous instrument." The danger lies in the harm that can be done by a golf ball in flight. However, the court does not suggest that a golf club in itself is a dangerous instrument. <u>Green</u> also is a different issue: the standard of care that a child should be held to if that child is engaging in an adult activity.

A second question involves the impact that <u>Green</u> makes to the question of David Peterson, Sr.'s liability in <u>Aarons</u>. Nothing in <u>Green</u> indicates that tools, like a golf ball in flight, would have to be considered dangerous instruments unless the nail in flight is analogous to the golf ball. However, golf balls are supposed to be hit to be in flight; a nail is not. One could even argue that a person has greater control using a hammer and nails than hitting a golf ball. Moreover, there is no custom in the use of tools similar to that of yelling "fore" in golf. Finally, <u>Green</u> does not indicate the extent of a <u>parent's</u> liability when that parent's child is engaging in an adult activity. <u>Green</u> is also based on a policy of keeping public golf courses safe.

Exercise 2-I: **Answer**

We have expanded the discussion on synthesizing cases because we think that it is both extremely important and difficult to master. To help the students

15

conceptually, we have identified three types of synthesis: grouping cases according to a rule they follow (the simplest kind of synthesis); defining the elements of an evolving claim or defense, (probably the most difficult kind of synthesis because it requires the student to work inductively to create an abstract theory); and identifying the factors that courts use to determine how a cause of action can be proven (probably the most common type of synthesis). We emphasize the importance of topic sentences to explain the case synthesis.

Cases 1 through 4 establish the principle that parents are immune from negligence suits brought by their minor children.

Cases 5 though 7 all deal with negligence suits. In cases 5 and 6, the children are dependent on their parents, even though they are over the age of majority. Their parents are, therefore, immune from suit. However, in case 7, the child is 20, lives away from home, and is emancipated. Under this circumstance, the parent is not immune from suit.

Therefore, the factors deciding parental immunity are:

1.   the type of tort (intentional tort or negligence)
2.   the age of the child
3.   whether the child was emancipated.

Exercise 2-J: Answer

This is an exercise for factor synthesis. We recommend this exercise; it doesn't have to take long, but can be expanded for an interesting discussion. Ask the students to identify the factors, one case at a time, and recharacterize them as you go through the list. Most students start naming factors as:

Case 1:   Time (after the robbery) - 1 day
                Distance (from murder) - 50 miles

Case 2:   Time and distance - moments later and close by

Case 3:   Time and distance - 1 hour distance, that courts use to
                determine how a cause of action can be proven, not
                known, but some distance
                Relationship between co-felons regarding original felony
                (new factor) - ongoing

16

Case 4:   Time - 2 hours
                 Distance - not known
                 Relationship - concluded (one felon in custody)

Case 5:   Time - 6 hours
                 Distance - not known
                 Relationship - concluded

Somewhere between Cases 3 and 5, we return to Cases 1 and 2 to add the "relationship" factor, and someone will decide that "distance" should be recharacterized as "continuing relationship." Often, after Case 5, someone will question whether "time" has any independent value. This question may lead to a discussion of which factors are important for the reason behind the "immediate flight" rule, and how to organize a discussion of the rule by these topics, rather than case by case.

You may also give the students the following synthesis[1] to evaluate, and ask what additional cases/facts they need to test it.

A defendant is in "immediate flight" if apprehended within an hour after the robbery was committed. If the time period is greater than an hour, then a defendant is in "immediate flight" if the defendants' collaboration is continuing after the murder. Collaboration can be continuing if proceeds will be shared after the murder.

Exercise 2-K: Answer

The factors from these cases could be the degree of intrusiveness into the defendant's home or person.

---

[1] Judy Rosenbaum, Assistant Director at Northwestern, wrote this synthesis.

Chapter Three

Analyzing Legal Authority: Statutes

This chapter completes our introductory materials on analyzing primary legal authority. If your students take a separate legal methods course, you may want to omit this chapter or parts of it.

This chapter begins with an explanation of the importance of reading statutes. It explains what the student should look for when reading the text of a statute, for example, definitions sections and how modifiers are used in the text. Although students may think it is simplistic beyond belief to be told to read the exact text of the statute, we are often amazed by their failure to do so. We then go on to exercises about finding and writing the statutory issues in a problem. In the third section of this chapter, we get into the more difficult problems of analyzing statutory language and determining legislative intent. The section provides an introduction to the various techniques of statutory interpretation. Chapter Eleven, III B, continues this discussion of analyzing statutes and includes other techniques of statutory analysis.

You may decide that the material in Part III is too difficult at this stage. If so, then consider assigning Parts I and II now. Or Parts I, II, and the first page of Part III. Then pick up the rest of the chapter later in the semester or the year, perhaps in combination with Chapter Eleven.

Although we explain what a legislative history is and when it is used, we have not delved into the recurring criticism that courts use legislative history too much and inappropriately. Justice Jackson's criticisms of using legislative histories to determine legislative intent are well known, see Schwegmann Bros. v. Calvert Distillers Corp., 341 U.S. 384 (1951); United States v. Public Utilities Commission, 345 U.S. 295 (1953). Justice Scalia more recently also expressed these criticisms, for example, in his concurring opinion when he was a judge on the D.C. Circuit in Hirschey v. Federal Energy Regulating Comm'n, 777 F.2d 1 (D.C. Cir. 1985), and in dissent in Johnson v. Transportation Agency, 480 U.S. 616 (1987) and Edwards v. Aguillard, 482 U.S. 578 (1987). In Hirschey, for example, Justice Scalia said,

> I frankly doubt that it is ever reasonable to assume that the details, as opposed to the broad outlines of purpose, set forth in a committee report come to the attention of, much less are approved by, the House which enacts the committee's bill. And I think it time for courts to become concerned about the fact that routine deference to the detail of committee

reports...[are] converting a system of judicial construction into a system of committee staff prescription.

777 F.2d at 7-8.

Justice Scalia also believes that the <u>Holy Trinity</u> case was wrongly decided. This case is explained on page 64 (the case about the church that hired an English minister), and is frequently used as an example of a court deciding a case by using legislative intent rather than plain meaning. Justice Scalia has described the outcome of this case as preposterous. "The act [hiring the minister] was within the letter of the statute, and was therefore within the statute. End of case." Quoted in Linda Greenhouse, <u>At the Bar</u>, N.Y. Times, March 17, 1995, at B 12.

Critics also are concerned with the costs that legislative histories impose and with the threat to democratic theory that they present (the judicial interpretation of a statute's legislative history can override the legislature's voice expressed in the statutory text). On the other hand, other critics have demonstrated the difficulties in determining plain meaning. *See* Chapter 11, Part III(A), Conference, *What is Meaning in a Legal Text? Northwestern University/Washington University Law & Linguistics Conference*, 73 WASH. U.L.Q. 769 (1995), and Lawrence S. Solan, "Learning Our Limits: The Decline of Textualism in Statutory Cases," 1997 WIS. L. REV. 235 (1997).

Exercise 3-A: Answer

1. Alternatives:	a dog or other animal
	damages another's property or injures any person
	damages or injury [optional] are same alternatives
2. Elements:	dog or other animal
	without provocation
	damages another's property or injures any person
	who is peacefully conducting himself
	where he may lawfully be.

You can combine into four elements as some courts have done.

"(1) damage caused by an animal owned by the defendant; (2) lack of provocation; (3) peaceable conduct of the person injured; and (4) the presence of the injured person in a place where he has a legal right to be."

Exercise 3-B: Answer

1.   Deceptive Collection Practices Act

      Facts 1:   This is a simple exercise, but shows students they must read statutory language and know the facts of their problem. The statute applies only to collection agencies, not to a private lender.

      Facts 2:   Oscar Green is an employee of a collection agency and the Deceptive collection Practices Act should apply to these facts as the section is written. Other information you would want to know is whether the Act applies to an agency employee's private loans, and to what amount of charge Green is entitled by law. People covering every base would want to first ascertain, of course, that Acme collection Agency is a "collection agency" within the Act.

2.   Animal Control Act

      Anderson is an "owner" under this statute because he has the animal in his care. Thus, he is not a "person" who can sue the owner for injuries under the same statute.

Exercise 3-C: Answers

      1.   Does a testator sign a will "in the presence" of a witness when the witness is in the next room at the time the testator signs?

      2.   Would a city "establish" a garbage dump within 250 yards of a residence by enlarging an existing dump with a newly purchased tract that is within 200 yards of a residence?

      3.   Are the decedent's adopted child and her non-marital child her "children" entitled to distribution of damages under the state's wrongful death statute?

      4.   Does a tennis teacher who is injured while playing tennis after work at his employer's premises with a patron of his employer's tennis facility suffer an injury "arising out of and in the course of employment?"

      5.   Does a dog act "without provocation" if the dog bites a child when another child is yelling because the dog has started barking?

Exercise 3-D: Answers

These have been done above.

Exercise 3-E: Answers

a.   The prosecutor has to prove that the defendant

-is a person
-who obtains "control"
-over property that has been "lost or mislaid"
-knew or learned the owner's identity, or knew of a reasonable method to learn the identity
-failed to restore the property through reasonable measures, and
-intended to permanently deprive the owner of the use of the property.

b.   The issues are:

-did Smith obtain control over the locket?
-was the locket lost or mislaid?
-did Smith know of a reasonable method of learning the identity of the locket's owner?
-did Smith fail to take reasonable measures to return the locket?
-did Smith intend to deprive the owner of the use of the property?

c.   The legally relevant facts are:

-Whether Smith obtained control

(1) Smith picked up the locket, looked it over, and put it in his pocket.

(2) About a block away from where he picked up the locket, someone took it from him.

-Whether the locket was lost or mislaid

(1) The locket was gold and was valuable, so probably would not have been intentionally left behind.

(2) The locket had a personal picture.

-Whether Smith knew of a reasonable method for identifying the owner of the locket

(1) Smith knew that the YWCA softball team had just practiced on the field where he found the locket.

(2) Smith may have known where the YWCA was located.

(3) The locket had three engraved initials.

These facts suggest that he could find out from the YWCA who on that team had those initials or lost the locket with these initials.

(4) Smith could also advertise in the newspaper for which he worked, or any other paper, or post signs in the park.

-Whether Smith failed to take reasonable measures to return the locket

(1) Smith put the locket in his pocket.

(2) Smith left the softball field in the opposite direction from the YWCA.

(3) Smith was robbed of the locket immediately upon leaving the park.

(4) Smith took no measures to return the locket during the time he had control, except to put the locket in his pocket. His possible intent seems irrelevant to this element.

-Whether Smith intended to deprive the owner of the use of the property

(1) Smith continued to work and left the park in the opposite direction from the YWCA.

(2) Smith's sister could use the locket because she had the same initials as those engraved on the locket.

Not many facts clearly show his intention. The inferences from these facts could be that he intended to deprive the owner of the locket. But he may have been planning to call the YWCA or bring the locket over later.

d. This assignment is suitable as an early short writing assignment. You may want to suggest that students look at Chapter Four, Large Scale Organization, for suggestions for organizing an analysis of a statute with elements. The organization should be quite simple: the statute's three elements preceded by the conditions that the defendant must have obtained control over the property and the property must have been lost or mislaid. You should tell your students if you want them to include a separate section of facts or if you want them to write the assignment assuming that the reader knows the facts.

Some suggestions for their analysis:

- Obtained control: the short time period is the problem here, but during that time period, Smith had authority over the locket.

-Lost or mislaid property: most students will assume that the locket was lost or mislaid, because most people will not purposely dispose of 14k jewelry, and because of the pictures, the owner probably had sentimental attachment to the locket.

- First element: The issue is whether Smith knew of a reasonable method of identifying the owner. The short time period of control isn't relevant here. Most students can suggest ways that Smith should have known, for example, call or go to the Y and get the list of team members, put up signs in the park, advertise, etc. The methods need not be successful, just reasonable.

- Second element: This one is harder to analyze, especially this early in the semester. One interpretation is that Smith took no measures to return the locket during the time he controlled it, except to put the locket in his pocket. If he took no measures, the state can prove this element of the statute. However, arguably, putting the locket in his pocket was a reasonable measure in those circumstances, to safeguard the locket until he could try to return it. If that is not enough (and few students identify this fact here) then another argument is that there were no reasonable measures that Smith could take because it would be unreasonable for him to interrupt his work in order to try to return the locket. Analysis that he may have intended to return the locket later is not relevant here.

- Third element: The students can use the facts set out above under part (c), and draw inferences from those facts as to Smith's intent. Most students agree that a prosecutor would not be able to prove beyond a reasonable doubt that Smith intended to permanently deprive the owner of the locket.

Exercise 3-F: Answers

This exercise is based on Right Reason Publications v. Silva, 691 N.E.2d 1347 (Ind. App. 1998).

1. The court interpreted the statutory terms narrowly and decided that the fair meaning of the word "school" does not include a university or college. The court used no extrinsic evidence. The university also is not a "community center." The court used a dictionary definition of "community" (a group of people living in the same locality and under the same government") to decide that a "community center" is a place to which the general public has access. The university involved here is a private one.

2. The journals were no longer Right Times's property because Right Times had abandoned them by putting them in the distribution stands, and had relinquished all property rights.

The court could have used a common meaning of "abandoned," but it relied on case law definitions and C.J.S.

Exercise 3-G: Answers

The first part of this exercise introduces students to the type of information they will find from legislative history materials. The examples given are the language from an earlier draft of the bill, a committee report excerpt, and a segment from the debate on the floor of the Senate, reported in the

Congressional Record. These sources discuss "confidential source" in terms of a human being.

The second part of the exercise provides arguments about why the legislative history is not necessarily dispositive of this issue. The speakers' references to individuals and their use of personal pronouns may not have been made with the precise distinction in mind between "confidential sources" as human beings and as non-human entities. The legislators may not actually have had the distinction in mind. The policy expressed in (c) and the statutory language may thus be important enough to override a somewhat ambiguous legislative history.

Exercise 3-H : Answers

The plaintiff's statutory argument is that the statute mandates that the department hold its hearing within thirty days of the plaintiff's request. Since the Department did not, its determination is void. The plaintiff can use <u>Adam</u> <u>v.</u> <u>Personnel Board</u> to support its interpretation of "shall" as mandatory.

The state's argument will be that "shall" is directory only. <u>Adam</u> arose under a different statute, and the state would argue that the court's reasoning there does not apply to TranQuil. The purpose of the Department's hearing is not necessarily to safeguard TranQuil's rights, but to safeguard those of its patients.

The plaintiff, however, would respond that its right to maintain its license is important enough to justify the interpretation of "shall" as directory.

You may want to discuss with your students the propriety of using the interpretation of "shall" from a different statute from the one at issue. Where the issue is the same and no purposes of the Personnel Code hearing prevent a party from using <u>Adam,</u> the definition can persuasively apply to the Nursing Home Act.

Exercise 3-I: Answer

1. The statutory definition of "debt" is broad, "any obligation . . . to pay money," and is not limited to payment on credit. A person who buys food is obligated to pay for it.

2. "Transaction" is not defined in the statute. The word may be ambiguous, but lack of a statutory definition will not by itself render a word ambiguous. Typically, the court will look first to the word's plain meaning. "Transaction" in the statute is limited to business dealings involving "personal, family, or household purposes," but not to credit as a means of payment.

3. That statement, if not refuted elsewhere, would be very definitive. However, see Question 4.

4. The FDCPA is part of the Consumer Credit Protection Act, which clearly applies to credit transactions only.

5. The court need not follow this decision because the issue in the other case was a different one, and the other court analyzed this issue with only one sentence. The court just noted the amendment's statutory structure.

This exercise is based on Bass v. Stolper, Koritzinsky, Brewster & Neider, S.C., 111 F.3d 1322 (7th Cir. 1997).

Exercise 3-J: Answers

1. This example is based on Lynch v. Donnelly, 465 U.S. 668 (1984) (Case 1) and American Jewish Congress v. Chicago, 827 F.2d 120 (7th Cir. 1987) (Case 2).

The Seventh Circuit held in American Jewish Congress that the holiday display violated the establishment clause. The court decided that the nativity scene was "self-contained" rather than just "one element of a larger display." The court reasoned that as a separate religious symbol, the scene advanced religion. The court also relied on another difference from the facts of Lynch: this display was in a government building and thus created the impression that the city endorsed religion.

2. This example is based on California v. Ciraolo, 471 U.S. 1134, reh'g. denied, 476 U.S. 207 (1986) (Case 1) and Florida v. Riley, 511 So. 2d 272 (Fla. 1987), rev'd, 488 U.S. 445 (1989). The Florida court distinguished Riley from Ciraolo because, using the helicopter, the police were able to hover and circle the defendant's premises at 400 feet and were able to look through openings of the defendant's roof and through the sides of the structure. The court decided that their observations were a greater intrusion on the defendant's reasonable expectation of privacy than surveillance from a fixed-wing aircraft at 1,000 feet

of a defendant's yard. The differences are the altitudes at which the police observed the defendant, the presence of the aircraft in navigable air space, the nature of the aircraft (a helicopter is markedly more maneuverable), and the difference between a yard and an enclosed building, the interior of which would not have been visible otherwise.

The plurality opinion of the United States Supreme Court reversed, however, on the grounds that the helicopter was within navigable airspace in which people routinely flew and any person could have legally been flying and observed the interior of the greenhouse through its open roof and sides.

Chapter Four

Organization of a Legal Discussion:
Large-Scale Organization

Most students find organizing a discussion very difficult. When they read a case or group of cases, they have trouble identifying the issues that are raised or even recognizing that issues are raised. If they have identified the significant issues, they may not know in which order to discuss them. As a result, their writing may be haphazard, their discussion may omit important points, and their work may be difficult to follow.

In this chapter we try to show students that the task of organizing a discussion is not a mysterious one. We suggest they analyze a claim for relief by breaking it down into its component parts. Where appropriate, they should then break each part down into its sub-parts. Finally, they should arrange these parts in logical order. When they have done this, they have organized their discussion.

We suggest first that the overall organization of a discussion is determined by the number of relevant claims or defenses. If a party is claiming both assault and battery, the discussion should be divided into two sections, one dealing with assault and one dealing with battery. If a party is defending against a breach of contract suit on the grounds of breach of warranties under the Uniform Commercial Code, then there could be three sections, one dealing with express warranty, one dealing with implied warranty of merchantability, and one dealing with implied warranty of fitness for a particular purpose. This basic division may be obvious to us, but it is not obvious to all students.

In the remainder of the chapter, we show students how to identify the issues raised by each claim. As we indicate in the introduction to this chapter, we use the word "issue" to mean the points that must be analyzed to determine the result under a particular claim. (This is different from the use of the word "issue" in the section in Chapter Two on briefing a case where "issue" refers to the basic question that the court has to decide.) It is useful to tell the students to organize their analysis by issues, not by cases. The general term "issue" can include the elements of a tort, the elements of a statute, and the general factors a court will consider in deciding a claim.

We then point out four ways in which students can find the issues:

1. A court's opinion identifies the elements of a rule.
2. The terms of a statute identify the elements.
3. The rule may evolve over a series of opinions.
4. The rule is vague and you must extract the factors from an opinion or a series of opinions and balance them.

If students realize that they can find the issues in a problem in these four basic ways, they should find the process of organizing a discussion less difficult. By making the process more systematic and less mysterious, we hope that we can help students with the difficult, but critically important, first step in analyzing a claim.

Throughout the chapter, we also note the considerations the students should keep in mind in deciding the order of issues: the existence of a threshold issue, the importance of an issue to the resolution of the problem, the complexity of the issues, and the dependence of one issue on the resolution of another issue. It is also worth noting that where a memo deals with two claims, one which has been specifically considered in the jurisdiction and one which has not, they should begin with the one that has been considered.   The chapter also discusses the organization of an analysis that involves balancing factors. Here, students can organize around either the factors, the parties to a dispute, or the judicial principles that guide an assessment of the factors.

We have followed a pattern in this chapter of first providing an example and analyzing that example for the students, and then providing an exercise which can be assigned as the basis of a classroom exercise. Depending on the length and complexity of the exercise, it can be either assigned as homework to be discussed in a later class, or read for the first time in class.

1.   The Court's Opinion Identifies the Elements of a Rule

It is often useful to give as a first writing assignment a problem in which one court opinion explicitly identifies the issues for the students. Tort problems work particularly well. The court may provide a definition, sometimes taken from the Restatement, that tells the students what the elements of a tort are. The court may even number the elements for the students, as the court has done in the Davis v. Finance Co. case. The students should see that each element constitutes an issue that must be analyzed. The text accompanying the example points out that issues do not necessarily merit equal attention and that students must decide the order in which they discuss the issues. Typically, however, they should analyze the elements in the order they appear in the definition of the claim, or explain why they are deviating from that pattern.

In the <u>Columbia River</u> case, we give the students an example of one opinion which includes all of the requirements for enforceability of covenants not to compete in that jurisdiction. The court also mentions the policy considerations which help explain the court's view. Unlike the tort cases discussed earlier in the chapter in which the court explicitly identifies the issues, in this type of case the student must extract and organize the issues with less help from the court. The suggested outline identifies the factors and gives reasons for discussing them in a particular order.

Exercise 4-A: Answer

The three elements in the tort of false imprisonment are:

1. an actor's intent to confine someone within boundaries fixed by the actor
2. a resulting confinement
3. the other person's consciousness of the confinement or harm by it

The court focuses its discussion on how the defendant may confine the plaintiff, which is by:

a. actual physical barriers
b. physical force
c. threat of physical force

The court further focuses its analysis on whether the plaintiff was confined by threat of physical force.

An outline of this problem would look something like this:

1. defendant's intent to confine
2. resulting confinement
   a. by physical barriers
   b. by physical force
   *c. by threat of physical force
3. plaintiff's consciousness of confinement or harm

Exercise 4-B: Answer

The court does not lay out the issues very clearly in this opinion, but they can be outlined as follows:

1.   Covenant must be ancillary to a valid contract, either

    a.   a valid written employment contract, or
    b.   a valid employment relationship,

and there must be

2.   Adequate consideration to support the covenant

and

3. Reasonable terms protecting legitimate business interests

    a.   geographic scope
    b.   temporal scope

2. The Terms of a Statute Identify the Elements

Statutory elements must be proven to enforce the statute. When students are analyzing a problem governed by a statute, they may not realize that the terms of the statute will identify the issues in their problem. Once they have identified the significant terms, they can make an outline of their analysis, using the terms as the basis for their organizational structure.

Students are directed to consider the overall structure of the statute in addition to the individual terms. We also suggest how to order and treat the issues.

Exercise 4-C: Answer

This exercise deals with a rather short and straightforward section of the Uniform Commercial Code, § 2-315 (a section discussed in the Sample Memorandum appended to the text).

The statute applies to buyers and sellers of goods (defined elsewhere in the Code). The time of contracting is the relevant time period. A warranty of fitness for a particular purpose is implied. The seller must know what the buyer's particular purpose is for the goods and that the buyer is relying on the seller's skill to provide suitable goods. The warranty can be excluded or modified as provided in the next section of the Code, § 2-316.

An outline of an analysis of this problem could look something like this:

A warranty of fitness for a particular purpose is implied if

    A.   at time of contracting

    B.   the seller
         -knows buyer's particular purpose and
         -knows buyer is relying on seller's skill or judgment
              -to select or furnish suitable goods

    C.   unless the warranty is modified or excluded under § 2-316

Exercise 4-D: Answer

An outline of the crime of burglary in the second degree, a more complex statute, could look something like this:

A. 1.   A person
      2.   knowingly enters a building unlawfully
               or
         knowingly remains unlawfully in a building
      3.   with intent to commit a crime

AND

B. 1.   in entry or immediate flight, he or another participant:
         a.   causes physical injury (very brief), or
         b.   is armed, or
         c.   uses or threatens immediate use of a dangerous instrument, or
         d.   displays a firearm

OR

2.   the building is a dwelling

3.   A Rule Evolves Over a Series of Cases

The most common and most difficult problems to organize are those in which the issues are not included in one opinion but must be extracted from a series of opinions. For example, after doing research on a simple problem, students may find 5 or 6 cases which deal with a claim for relief similar to the one with which they are working. The students may decide that the facts of one of these cases are so different that the case is not relevant. However, each of the other cases may, in varying degrees, contribute to their understanding of the topic. A case may state the basic rule and focus on one or more factors that courts will consider in analyzing this topic. Other cases may add to the basic standard. To organize their discussion, the students must identify the basic rule, that is, all of the elements that courts have come to require in analyzing this topic.

In the example dealing with negligent infliction of emotional distress, the Sinn case sets out the basic rule giving the factors that courts should consider in evaluating a plaintiff's claim, and a set of facts which illustrate this tort. The other cases elaborate on those factors or add new elements.

Exercise 4-E: Answer

The general rule is that non-resident parties and witnesses in civil actions are immune from service of process. The purpose for the rule is to assure the due administration of justice and to expedite the courts' business. It is not designed to protect the individual. Rather, it is intended to encourage the attendance of people whose attendance is necessary for a fair trial by providing them with an incentive to appear.

Courts will deny immunity under the following circumstances:

1.   Where both cases arise out of the same transaction (the reason for granting immunity is outweighed by the importance of resolving the full dispute between the parties)
2.   Where someone is in the jurisdiction as a defendant in a criminal action (an incentive is unnecessary since that person has no choice but to appear)
3.   Where someone is in the jurisdiction to serve his own interests (any other incentive is unnecessary)

An outline of an analysis of immunity from service of process would look something like this:

A. General rule - grant immunity
    Purpose   - not to protect individual
                          - to expedite courts' business and the administration of justice
                          - to provide incentive

B. Exceptions
    1. same transaction - reason
    2. criminal defendant - reason
    3. serve own interest - reason

4. The Rule is Vague and You Must Extract the Factors From an Opinion or a Series of Opinions and Balance Them

The last section of this chapter teaches students how to organize a totality of circumstances analysis. The student must determine which factors are legally relevant, how to characterize the factors, and which are the most important in order to determine whether a claim has been proven. Here again, we have suggested different organizing principles. One organization is to take each factor separately, perhaps in the order they are listed by the courts. Another method, especially useful when there are many factors to consider, is to group the factors around guiding principles suggested by the court. Students may also organize around parties, looking at the factors that favor each.

In the *Elliott v. Krear* case, we give the students an example of one opinion which includes all of the factors courts consider relevant to determining the domicile of a child. The court also mentions the policy considerations which help explain the court's view. A policy organization is a good organization for this problem.

Sometimes the factors emerge over a series of cases, as discussed in our example of what makes a contract unconscionable. Sometimes the factors are set out in a statute, as they are in the custody statute discussed in the text. There a party organization might be appropriate.

34

Exercise 4-F : Answer

"Physical custody," as interpreted by the courts, means something more than physical control. Merely having possession of the child is not enough. The <u>Peters</u> case shows that the child must be turned over voluntarily. Fortuitous actual custody is not enough to establish physical custody or the Act would encourage kidnapping. Furthermore, the child must be relinquished by the parent for more than a short time. The intent of the parent may not control as to whether the child was turned over temporarily or permanently, and must be balanced against family stability. In the case of Barbara, the court decided that temporary control was not enough to establish physical custody. However, in <u>Mennan</u>, the court held that the grandparents had physical custody after 7 years, even though Mennan had probably intended to turn the child over only temporarily, and had removed the child from their care when he returned after 7 years. Thus the factors are the manner by which the nonparent came to have physical possession of the child, the duration of the possession, and the nature of the possession.

Exercise 4-G: Answer

The basic standard that courts use in determining whether a hospital is liable for the suicide of one of its patients is whether the hospital used such reasonable care as the patient's known mental condition required. The hospital's duty is proportionate to the patient's needs. (<u>Ross</u>)

The factors courts will consider in determining a hospital's liability include:

1. the patient's mental history, including the frequency and proximity of suicide attempts (<u>Ross</u>, <u>Moore</u>, <u>Brown</u>)

2. observation by nurses (<u>Smith</u>, <u>Moore</u>)

3. the setting in which care was given - open vs. closed ward, precautions taken with regard to room and equipment (<u>Moore</u>, <u>Brown</u>)

4. the doctor's prognosis - seriousness of condition (<u>Ross</u>, <u>Smith</u>, <u>Moore</u>, <u>Brown</u>).

Chapter Five

Organization of a Legal Discussion:
Small-Scale Organization

Chapter Five attempts to demonstrate how the analytic skills discussed in Chapters One to Three are combined and ordered in a legal discussion. Part I of Chapter Five should be assigned before your students write their first closed universe problem. Part II should be assigned before the first research problem since it discusses case synthesis.

If you have designed a totality of circumstances problem or a problem that requires students to balance competing interests or policies, you may want to assign Part II, B(4) of Chapter Four, which will help your students to understand and organize that type of analysis.

The first exercise is not particularly difficult. It involves constructing an argument on a single issue using only one case as precedent and one hypothetical set of facts. You might be able to do it in class, for example, in small groups. The students could also do it at home, and you could discuss the responses in class.

The second exercise is probably too long to do in class. It involves writing an analysis of an issue that has three subissues and requires students to use a set of facts and the summaries of five cases as precedents. You could perhaps do it in class if you ask the students only to outline the discussion, telling students to choose the cases relevant to each subissue and list the pertinent facts and reasoning from the precedents and the problem case.

Exercise 5A: Answer

Discussion of Reckless Conduct

The second element of intentional infliction of emotional distress requires the plaintiff to show the defendant's conduct was intentional or at least reckless. Reckless conduct is established when it is a highly probable that the plaintiff will suffer severe emotional distress and the actor goes ahead in conscious disregard of it. Davis. Augusta gave Olympia clear warning that its conduct could result in severe emotional distress, but Olympia may not have consciously disregarded Augusta's warning.

In <u>Davis</u>, Finance Corp. did not act recklessly because it responded to Davis's warning that its conduct was causing severe distress. <u>Davis</u>. Finance Corp. stopped calling on Davis at the hospital during her visits to her ailing daughter after Davis told Finance Corp. that its appearances endangered her daughter's recovery. This situation also caused great anxiety and concern to the mother. Moreover, although Finance Corp. ignored Davis's later notice to Finance that its conduct was driving her "nuts," the court stated this was an insufficient showing of recklessness because Finance Corp. could not infer from this colloquialism that there was a high degree of probability that Davis would suffer severe emotional distress from a continuation of its collection tactics.

Livia Augusta gave Olympia a much more explicit and detailed account of the distress she was experiencing than Davis gave Finance Corp. when Davis warned she was going "nuts." During several phone calls, Augusta informed Olympia personnel that they were causing her insomnia, nightmares, and weight loss. She also wrote the president of Olympia warning him of her distress.

> The conduct of your personnel in pursuing payment for a purchase I never made is having a horrendous impact on my health and emotional stability. My physician is giving me tranquillizers around the clock to control the acute anxiety I have been experiencing. This situation is intolerable, and I expect you, as president of the store, to clear this matter up before I become a complete wreck.

Thus, Olympia cannot claim ignorance of the stress it was causing.

A more difficult question is whether Olympia recklessly disregarded Augusta's warning. Olympia's president promised to resolve Augusta's billing problem, but warned her that it might take "a week or so." It is quite possible that the letter informing Augusta that she had been reported to the Credit Rating Bureau was written before the President had a chance to attend to this matter. On the other hand, Olympia's president may have recklessly delayed attending to Augusta's problem. Instead of acting within a week, he waited over two weeks, despite Augusta's warning that her mental condition was perilous. Given the situation, Augusta can probably establish that Olympia acted recklessly.

Exercise 5B: Answer

Discussion of Severe Distress

The third element of intentional infliction of emotional distress requires the plaintiff to show her distress is severe. <u>Davis</u>. Although symptoms such as "fright, horror, grief, shame, humiliation, or worry may fall within the ambit of the term emotional distress," these mental conditions must be so severe that a reasonable person could not endure them. Id. In addition, the plaintiff must establish that defendant's actions were the cause-in-fact of the distress. Dale. Because Augusta's mental stability has steadily and significantly deteriorated since Olympia began its harassment, Augusta can probably satisfy this element of the tort.

One factor the court scrutinizes in determining whether the plaintiff's mental condition is such that no reasonable person could be expected to endure it is whether the plaintiff is able to function in his or her professional and personal life. Histrionic; Dale. In Histrionic, the court found that plaintiff's behavior-- ranting, weeping, tantrum throwing--was "consistent with his prior character and professional training," did not interfere unduly in his daily functioning. Histrionic. In contrast, the Dale court said in dicta that Dale's distress fell within the ambit of the term severe distress, although it held that the plaintiff failed to show defendant's actions were the cause-in-fact of plaintiff's distress. Dale. Dale's depression made him unable to function as a caring husband to his seriously ill wife and as a man responsibly seeking employment.

Although Augusta's anxiety seems less disruptive than Dale's depression, her mental condition has had a greater effect on her job performance and personal life than Histrionic's had. Her trouble concentrating and her unfortunate nap during a business conference led her employer to warn her to "shape up." In addition, her fatigue has forced her to forego socializing in the evening. Because Augusta cannot control her anxiety without tranquillizers, and because her treatment seems to impede her normal functioning, she should prove this factor.

The second factor courts scrutinize in determining whether the distress is severe is the condition's impact on the person's physical health and emotional welfare. Marlboro. The depression that June Marlboro experienced as a result of defendant's harassment posed such a serious threat to her mental and physical health that the court found no reasonable person could endure it. Id. See also Dale (emotional paralysis requiring anti-depressants satisfied factor). Augusta's distress does not yet pose a serious threat to her long-term health. Nonetheless, Augusta is worried about the effect daily dosages of valium may have on her health. Moreover, her emotional well being has already suffered. Her bouts of hyperventilation, her insomnia, her weight loss, and her nightmares leave her feeling continually fatigued and frightened. Given the anxiety Augusta experiences and its effect upon her physical and emotional health, a court would probably find Augusta's distress severe.

38

Augusta should have no problem showing that Olympia's actions were the cause-in-fact of her distress. <u>See</u> <u>Dale</u>. Whereas Jim Dale's depression could have been caused by any one of the traumas confronting him--his wife's fatal disease, his unemployment, or New City Hospital's collection methods--Augusta faces no trauma other than Olympia`s harassment. Moreover, her distress began only after the store's harassment, and the link between Olympia's phone calls and Augusta's worst attacks of anxiety and hyperventilation is immediate and consistent. Thus, Augusta can satisfy all the requirements that establish severe distress.

Chapter Six

The Thesis Paragraph

Chapter Six completes our introduction to legal method, legal analysis, and legal writing. The chapter stresses the importance of establishing the context of a discussion and suggests the kinds of information a reader would find helpful in an introduction. The chapter can be read and the exercises done after the first five chapters have been covered, especially Chapter Four on identifying the issues, and just before you assign your students an objective analysis like a memorandum. You could also do the exercises earlier if, for example, you are assigning an early para-legal type exercise and have given the students the issues.

Because the exercises are short, they can be done in class, either individually or in small collaborative groups. Leave class time for comparing and evaluating the responses.

If students write conclusions rather than brief answers for their office memos, you may want them to write a briefer introductory paragraph that provides the legal context, but not necessarily an application of the rule/s or a conclusion.

Exercise 6-A: Answers

1.   Thesis paragraph B is a better introductory paragraph than thesis A. Thesis A does not state the legal question clearly, namely, that domicile is important for establishing diversity jurisdiction. Although the tests established by Ferrara are set forth and the significant facts of the precedent given, the relevant facts from the problem case are omitted, and the conclusion is, therefore, unsubstantiated. Thesis B clearly sets out the legal issue, controlling rules, supporting facts, and conclusion.

2.   Thesis paragraph B is a clearer introductory paragraph than thesis A. The topic sentence in thesis A is legally incorrect. Moreover, although two of the tests for intentional infliction of distress are set forth in thesis A, the writer does not make it clear that the severity of distress is also a factor. Moreover, the writer fails to include relevant facts and fails to offer a legal conclusion. The topic sentence of thesis B explicitly states the cause of action. The standards are clearly listed, and facts supporting the legal conclusion are thoughtfully summarized.

3.   A thesis paragraph for the John Starr and Alice Doe problem might look as follows:

To sustain a suit against the Pennsylvania Deluxe Hotel for negligent infliction of emotional distress, John Starr and Alice Doe must satisfy four requirements. First, they must be closely related to the victim. John is Jane's husband, and Alice is Jane's great aunt and tacit mother. Thus, they have this requisite relationship. Second, their shock must result from a single, identifiable traumatic event. The trauma of witnessing Jane being shot is the sole cause of John's and Alice's shock. Third, the plaintiffs must suffer severe emotional distress. This factor can also be satisfied: Alice had a breakdown; John was so distraught he was unable to work for three months and unable to handle his anxiety about his wife. More problematic is the requirement that the plaintiffs be near enough to the scene of the accident that the shock results from its sensory and contemporaneous observance. John and Alice saw the accident on T.V. rather than in person. Nonetheless, they did not learn of the shooting after the fact, but saw it on the screen as it was happening. Thus, John and Alice can probably satisfy this factor also and recover for the negligent infliction of emotional distress.

or

To sustain a suit against the Pennsylvania Deluxe Hotel for negligent infliction of emotional distress, John Starr and Alice Doe must satisfy four requirements. First, the plaintiffs must be closely related to the victim. Second, their shock must result from a single, identifiable traumatic event. Third, the plaintiffs must suffer severe emotional distress. Fourth, the plaintiffs must be near enough to the scene of the accident that their shock results from its sensory and contemporaneous observance. John and Alice should have little difficulty satisfying the first three elements of this tort. The fourth requirement is more problematic because the plaintiffs saw the incident on T.V. rather than in person. Nonetheless, there was no buffer against the full impact of the event. They did not learn of the shooting after the fact, but saw it on the screen as it was happening. Thus, John and Alice can probably satisfy this factor also and recover for the negligent infliction of emotional distress.

Chapter Seven

Writing a Legal Document: The Legal Memorandum

With this chapter, we apply more specifically the legal method skills of the early chapters to writing legal documents.   Since the intra-office memorandum is the most commonly used assignment for first-year legal writing courses, this chapter explains how to organize and write a legal memorandum. We go into some detail about the function that each part serves within a memo and give examples of good and bad writing. We have tried to include text or examples drawn from common student mistakes. A Check List for students is at the end of the chapter.

This chapter briefly and generally explains the Discussion section of the memorandum. The previous chapters discuss in detail how to organize and write a legal discussion. We also briefly raise the topic of writing clearly. Chapters Nine and Ten discuss in detail how to write clear sentences and coherent paragraphs and Appendix A includes rules of grammar and punctuation. Chapter Eight explains how to put all this information together in a first memorandum.

Exercise 7-A: Answers

Example 1 is the best Statement of Facts. The first paragraph establishes the context of the problem. The second paragraph includes the facts relevant to Wheeler's intent to change domicile to Connecticut. This is really a topical organization rather than a chronological one. The last paragraph explains the issue that the writer has been asked to analyze, an important inclusion here in order to distinguish the topic from the substantive malpractice issue.

Example 2 begins with the potential defendant rather than with the writer's client. This example is confusing. It includes facts that are irrelevant to the diversity jurisdiction issue and the writer does not clearly explain what question the memo has been limited to.

Example 3 begins as a chronological account of the facts instead of setting out the context of the problem. The writer continues chronologically, including facts relevant to the jurisdiction issue, but has never identified what he has been asked to do.

Exercise 7-B: Answers

1. This QP sets out the cause of action and the crucial facts, but the question is somewhat slanted against the attorney.

This conclusion supplies an answer but the writer does not have to say "applying the precedents to this case." The reader assumes that is what an attorney will do to analyze the problem. In addition, this conclusion omits one of the facts set out in the question (the attorney's past failure to appear), and it does not link the facts it does mention to the controlling legal standard.

2. The QP is not written in terms of the client, but written as if the issue were a definition of criminal contempt. However, the definition is well settled.

The conclusion supplies the definition, although poorly, but gives no reason for the predicted outcome. Thus, this pair sets out the controlling rule but does not apply the rule to the facts.

3. This pair is the best. The QP sets out the cause of action and the relevant facts. The conclusion answers the QP, specifically refers to the facts raised in the QP, and links them to the legal standard for criminal contempt.

4. The QP asks a question that the case law has already answered affirmatively. The issue should be under what circumstances is an attorney guilty if he did not appear. This question also does not include any facts of the case.

The conclusion contains a common student problem, that of not answering the question. This conclusion is a variant of "it's all up to the court," or "it depends on what the jury decides." The conclusion also includes some unnecessary jargon in the form of "so act."

Chapter Eight

The Writing Process

This chapter responds to what most students identify as their most difficult task in the first part of the course: putting together a memorandum for the first time. We find that even when we use short assignments that build up to the first memo, the memo is a daunting experience. Thus, you may want to assign this chapter when you assign your first memorandum. The chapter breaks down the steps from pre-writing through editing to give students a sense of the whole process. We provide specific suggestions for each phase of the process, suggestions that apply not only to memos, but also to many other forms of writing. This chapter has several examples, but no exercises.

The chapter is structured in linear fashion, but it is a good idea to advise students that they may need to go back and forth between the stages.

In Part II, Beginning Your Assignment, we provide students with suggestions on how to read their assignments and the materials. When reading, they should identify the controlling rule(s), notice how that rule is broken down into elements or factors (you may want to relate this stage to the large-scale organization in Chapter Four), and begin to think about how the rule(s) play out against the facts of the cases.

In Part III, From Research to Outline, we go into detail about how to create an outline based on these topics rather than an outline based on individual cases. The "topics" are the controlling rule(s) and its constituent parts (elements, factors, etc.), that is, we stress organizing by issues, not by cases. We provide an example of a simple bare-bones outline and of two more complete outlines, using procedural unconscionability and the contact element of a battery claim. We relate these outlines to the material on small-scale organization in Chapter Five.

Part IV is about writing the first draft and explains the technique known as freewriting. Students who have prepared a detailed outline can get their first draft on paper (or screen) by writing from that outline. Those students who do not outline or write from their outline will find these freewriting suggestions helpful not only to get words on paper or screen, but to analyze as they go. Part IV also offers suggestions about the order in which to write the sections of a memo as well as techniques to try when the writing bogs down.

The last part of the chapter is on rewriting. We suggest students edit in stages, focusing first on the analysis, and then in turn on organization and sentence structure. It is important to emphasize that spell checking programs are an aid to proofreading, but do not replace the task.

Chapter Nine

Effective Paragraphs

This chapter can be assigned at any time, in part or in total. The first three sections--on topic sentences and paragraph unity, transitions, and paragraph coherence--are central to good writing. The exercises are relatively easy and can be done in class, either in small groups or individually. Exercise 9-C is an editing and review exercise. The student is asked to edit a discussion based on Exercise 2-H(1) in Chapter Two. You might want to do 2-H(1) and 9-C in conjunction with each other.

Exercise 9A: Answers

1.	A topic sentence unifying <u>Dale</u> and <u>Histrionic</u> might look as follows:

> One factor the court scrutinizes in determining whether a plaintiff's mental condition is such that no reasonable person could be expected to endure it is whether the plaintiff is able to function in his or her professional life.

2.	A topic sentence unifying cases 5, 6, and 7 might look as follows:

> Even if a child has arrived at the age of majority, parents are immune from that child's negligence suit against them if that child still lives at home and is dependent.

3.	**Paragraph 1 -** The thesis paragraph is fine.

	Paragraph 2 - The paragraph should not begin with the facts of <u>Kramer</u> but with a topic sentence on the principle the case establishes. The information in the last sentence could work as the first sentence.

Example

> A merely possible connection between the defendant's negligence and the plaintiff's injury is not enough to permit a jury to consider whether the negligence caused the injury. <u>Kramer Services Inc. v. Wilkins</u>.

| **Paragraph 3 -** | The paragraph would benefit from a transition that weighs Warren's claim against the decided case. |

Example

Ellen Warren will be able to present substantially more and better evidence of causation than Wilkins could.

| **Paragraph 4 -** | This paragraph needs a transition sentence introducing the opposing argument. |

Example

However, Ellen Warren's family has a hereditary history of cancer, and the defendants may argue that Ellen Warren's hereditary susceptibility to cancer may have caused her cancer.

| **Paragraph 5 -** | This paragraph also needs a transition sentence. |

Example

It will be harder to show that DES is more than a merely possible cause of Warren's infertility and miscarriage, as opposed to her cancer.

Exercise 9-B: Answers

1. This paragraph would have a more logical organization if it started with the broad legal principle.

Because a waiver of the right to counsel may not be lightly inferred, Ledbetter v. State, 581 P. 2d 1129, 1131 (Alaska 1978), the degree of the court's inquiry must be tailored to the particular characteristics of the accused. O'Dell v. Anchorage, 576 P. 2d 104, 108 (Alaska 1978). In some cases a defendant may be permitted to waive his right without detailed inquiry. Kelly v. State, 663 P.2d 967, 969 (Alaska Ct. App. 1983). In Kelly, the court found that the defendant, who had demonstrated a long and broad experience with the legal process, had knowingly and intelligently waived counsel, although the trial judge had made no detailed inquiry. Id. Here, Miller stated that his mother had married an attorney after his father's death; his mother's marriage cannot, however, be construed as meaningful legal experience for Miller.

47

Furthermore, unlike Miller, Kelly availed himself of some of the services of court appointed counsel while defending himself. Id.

2.   Transition words improve this paragraph's coherence.

The degree of judicial inquiry will also depend on the complexities and gravity of the legal issues raised by the charge against the defendant. O'Dell v. Anchorage, 576 P.2d 104, 108 (Alaska 1978). For example, traffic misdemeanor cases are easily understood by lay persons, and the consequences are usually not severe. Id. Thus the inquiry in such cases need not be extensive. Id. However, Miller, if convicted, faces a mandatory jail term and not a simple parking fine. The severity of these charges mandated a more extensive inquiry by the judge.

3.   Connectors and sentence overlapping improve this paragraph's coherence.

Whether the state's suppression of evidence in a criminal prosecution violates the defendant's due process rights depends on four conditions. First, the state must be responsible for the loss of the evidence. Second, the evidence must have had exculpatory value that was apparent before it was lost. Third, the defendant has been unable to obtain comparable evidence by any other reasonable means. Finally, if the evidence was only potentially exculpatory, the defendant must demonstrate that it was lost due to bad faith on the part of the state. Here, Roger Keith can show that the state was responsible for the loss of the alleged murder weapon, the car. However, because the car disappeared from the police garage before it was examined, its exculpatory value was never demonstrated. Therefore, it would be difficult to determine what comparable evidence might consist of. In addition, the record offers little to prove that the loss of the potentially exculpatory car was due to bad faith on the part of the police. Because Keith likely will not meet the conditions for determining violation of his due process rights because of state suppression, the court will most likely deny the motion for dismissal.

4.   Your students might have trouble re-organizing this paragraph because they are uncertain what legal point the writer is trying to make. Thus, you might want to use this exercise to illustrate the interdependence of substance and paragraph organization and coherence. Until a writer is clear about the focus of a paragraph, it is difficult to

order sentences and make effective transitions. The point of the paragraph is clearer in the following rewrite.

If a person uses an extension telephone within "the ordinary course of business," then the person does not unlawfully intercept the defendants' communication. When there are several extension phones, as there are in the orderly room, it is not unusual that when a call comes in, a person will pick up the receiver to see who the call is for. The parties agree that First Sergeant Valiant of C. Company first picked up the phone to learn who was being called. During the first few seconds after picking up the phone, Valiant overheard a conversation between members of his Company that began "Do you have any of the good stuff?" He recognized the speakers, who were later court martialed on drug charges. <u>Because</u> the sergeant picked up the phone in the ordinary course of business, he did not "intercept" the conversation.

Exercise 9-C: Answer

Edit of <u>Peterson</u> Response

wordy and imprecise statement of the issue

The issue ~~that we must explore in this case~~ is ~~the question~~ *David Peterson is liable in negligence for injuries inflicted on a nine-year-old child* whether ~~the father is responsible for the injuries resulting from his~~ *when Peterson's son attempted to use tools Peterson had stored in the basement.*

tentative and wordy

~~son's misuse of a hammer.~~ (The applicable rule would be that) a *cite*

good

person has a duty to protect other against <u>unreasonable</u> risks. A

person who breaches this duty is negligent and liable for injuries

Peterson did not create an unreasonable risk because tools stored in the basement are not

Who left the tools? Tools were stored, not left.

resulting from his negligence. ~~It must be shown that leaving the~~ "*obviously and intrinsically dangerous*" *as required in Smith v. Allen.*

Give your conclusion.

~~tools in the basement was an unreasonable risk.~~

Although David Peterson

You need a topic sentence on the subject of the paragraph

(In the present case, the father) left his tools in the *cite*

basement, Tools are not "obviously and intrinsically dangerous."

omit - this is obvious

(The case must be discussed in light of relevant precedent. The

legalese

<u>Smith</u> case clearly applies to the case herein) In <u>Smith</u>, the court

49

sustained defendant's demurrer ~~to the complaint,~~ challenging the sufficiency of the complaint. In Smith, the children were playing with a golf club. Many similarities obviously can be pointed out between Smith and the present case. The children were identical in age. The instruments were left in an area played in by children, the accidents occurred without warning the victims.

Plaintiff herein may claim that the tools should not have been left where children could reach them. Defendant may state that in Smith, the golf club was left in the backyard, also a play area for children. The golf club ~~was not held~~ to be intrinsically dangerous. We must also be concerned with whether tools, although not inherently dangerous, can be considered more dangerous in the hands of a child than a golf club. Tools are like a golf club ~~because they~~ are not weapons; ~~however~~, they may be misused by a child.

Give holding first so we know why it matters

misplaced modifier, goes with demurrer

be precise

avoid

wordy - try "exist"

Need transition. e.g. "For example"

transition (In both cases)

semi-colon

point unclear

who?

too emotional

legalese

Clarify plaintiff's argument before switching to defendant. Is it that objects that children misuse are intrinsically dangerous when left in a play area? Evaluate that argument.

However,

court had that the

active voice

because?

wordy, unnecessary

wordy

"may be" =

This is a slightly separate point from the one in the first paragraph

=

although

Don't skip from one subject (location) to another (dangerousness).

Chapter Ten

Sentence Structure

This chapter discusses principles of syntax and diction. Exhaustive treatment of these topics is beyond the scope of this book. We have, however, tried to discuss those principles of sentence structure with which students frequently have trouble. The chapter can be assigned at any time. It can also be used as a reference chapter. When you edit student work, you can make marginal comments on sentence errors that refer students to the relevant number and discussion in the text. For punctuation errors, key your comments to Appendix A.

The answers to the exercises in Chapter Ten begin on the next page. You may wish to photocopy and distribute them to your students.

Exercise 10-A: Answers

1. Dangling modifier (the subject doing the calculating does not appear in the sentence).   Passive voice.

    Answer:
    In calculating damages, the jury considered the rehabilitation costs to be the greatest expense.

2. Faulty parallelism.

    Answer:
    The drug companies can either insure themselves against liability, absorb the damage awards, or pass the cost along to the public.

3. Keep the subject of the sentence near the predicate.   Eliminate the interrupting phrases. Break into two sentences.

    Answer:
    Canon 9 reflects the Bar's concern with protecting the integrity of the legal system by prohibiting both impropriety and the mere appearance of impropriety. Canon 9 alone is a basis for sustaining a disqualification motion.

4. Misplaced modifier.

    Answer:
    Heated arguments over technicalities had often occurred in the middle of negotiation.

5. Passive voice.

    Answer:
    The defendant requested a jury trial.

6. Comparative sentences require two terms.

    Answer:
    Keith Johnson's case is more factually similar to *Ziady v. Curley* than to *Elliot v. Krear*.

7.   Misplaced modifier (the court, not the letter, emphasized).

       Answer:
       The court admitted into evidence the decedent's letter charging her
       husband with cruelty, indifference, and failure to support. It emphasized
       that admitting the letter did not violate the statutory rule.

8.   Passive voice. Nominalization.

       Answer:
       A court determines whether to award consequential damages according
       to the facts of each case.

9.   Faulty Parallelism

       Answer:
       The state interest in setting a filing fee is to raise revenue and to
       deter unmeritorious use of judicial time.

10.   Comparative sentences must compare similar things

       Answer:
       Unlike the mother in *Elliot*, Keith's mother had never relinquished
       custody.

11.   Empty introduction. Avoid the "it must be shown", "it can be shown"
       syndrome.

       Answer:
       The plaintiff must suffer or have suffered emotional distress in order to
       state a claim.

12.   Begin a sentence with a short specific subject instead of a long subject.

       Answer:
       A dangerous instrument is any instrument, article, or substance which,
       under the circumstances in which it is used, is capable of causing death
       or serious injury.

13.   Remove interrupting phrases and clause that separate the subject and
       verb.

Answer:
Knowing the prosecutor had the authority of the government behind her, and aware of her access to the files, the jury gave her words great weight.

14. Edit for sexist language.

Answer:
The proscription against a prosecutor expressing a personal opinion goes to the heart of a fair trial.

15. Edit for nominalization.

Answer:
The McCaren-Ferguson Act exempts the business of insurance.

16. Edit for nominalization and ambiguous use of passive voice.

Answer:
A landlord can breach an implied warranty of habitability even without violating city building and housing codes.

17. Faulty parallelism

Answer:
The landlord agrees to provide heat, pay for all utilities, maintain an air-conditioning system, and keep the premises in good order.

Exercise 10-B: Answers

1. Faulty parallelism.

    Answer:
    A social host may be liable for the consequences of a guest's drunken driving if the host directly serves the alcohol, continues serving after the guest is visibly drunk, and knows that the guest will soon be driving home.

2. Wrong word. ("Drastically" has the wrong connotation for an affirmative development.)

    Answer:
    Her innovative programming dramatically increased attendance at the youth programs.

3. Length. (Too many tacked on modifiers. Divide into two or three sentences.) Use *that* for restrictive modifier. Add transitions.

    Answer:
    The firm entered into a two-year contract with Ms. Taylor. **During these years**, she introduced several new products **that** increased sales. **Moreover**, her work earned her an "employee of the year" award.

4. Misplaced modifier.

    Answer:
    By silencing you, your teacher violated your first amendment rights.

5. Keep the subject near the verb.

    Answer:
    In dismissing Mann's complaint under Rule 12(b)(6) of the federal Rules of Civil Procedure, the trial court stated that it was not necessary to decide the merits of defendant's argument.

6. Avoid subject phrases. Start with a short specific noun.

    Answer:
    The second requirement is that the defendant acted with deliberate indifference.

7. Faulty parallelism.

    Answer:
    Robertson granted visitation rights to Ms. Cavallo after she had committed heinous acts of abuse against Julia, abandoned her, and abused another child.

8. Wordy.

    Answer:
    Although settlement may result in less compensation than if you prevail at a formal hearing, it is a much quicker and more flexible process.

9. Subject phrase. Wordy.

    Answer:
    A church is shielded from state laws only if the court would become excessively entangled in inherently ecclesiastical matters by enforcing those laws.

10. Dangling modifier. Passive voice.

    Answer:
    By firing you, your employer violated the contract.

11. Compare like things.

    Answer:
    Such neutrality on the part of Utopia's School District cannot be compared to the conduct of the Districts in *Lee, Engel,* and *Abington.*

12. Misplaced modifier.

    Answer:
    On August 3, Julia was born prematurely and shortly thereafter began suffering withdrawal symptoms associated with drug addiction.

13.   Wordy

Answer:
Should these matters go to trial, the Board may have to pay compensatory and punitive damages.

Chapter Eleven

Types of Legal Arguments in
Resolving Questions of Law

This chapter explains types of legal analysis prominent in questions of law. Some of this material was covered in earlier chapters, such as broad and narrow interpretation, and statutory interpretation using both the plain meaning rule and legislative intent. We also briefly discussed the importance of policy in interpreting the law. In this chapter we discuss these concepts in greater depth and at a somewhat more complex level. For example, we discuss forms of syntactic and semantic ambiguity that complicate plain meaning analysis in Part III A. We have a full discussion of types of legal arguments used in both common law and statutory questions of law and a full discussion of the policy arguments that frequently occur in legal discourse.

The examples and exercises are concerned with identifying and organizing these arguments. Until students become adept at recognizing different types of argument, they will have trouble creating and rebutting them. Another point to stress is that often several types of arguments are relevant to an issue and students must marshal these arguments in order to reach a convincing conclusion; just analyzing a few cases is not enough.

The statutory arguments are frequently illustrated with a discussion of Bragdon v. Abbott, 118 S. Ct. 2196 (1998), in which the Court held that people infected with HIV are protected from discrimination under the Americans with Disabilities Act even if they suffer no symptoms of AIDS. The extensive legislative history of the ADA and its predecessor statute, the Rehabilitation Act of 1973, as well as the Court's plain meaning analyses made this case a good example of a variety of interpretative arguments.

The policy arguments are illustrated with a hypothetical case that asks a court to recognize a new cause of action for loss of parental consortium. A number of different policy concerns factor into a decision on this issue. In discussing policy arguments, you may want to remind students that policy arguments are often made in the context of other arguments and are not separated out.

Exercise 11-A: Answers

1.   Enter . . . in a building

2.   Defendant's and State's arguments by type.

<u>Smith</u>

a) statutory interpretation:
   plain meaning

b) common law argument:
   narrow interpretation
   of precedents

c) statutory interpretation:
   Legislative intent and
   policy (purpose of statute)

<u>State</u>

a) common law argument:
      precedent extends to new situation
      (even if he didn't <u>enter</u> the building,
      the policy extends to the premises)

b) statutory argument: plain meaning
      and canon of construction

c) common law argument: broad
      interpretation of precedents

Outline of order of arguments:

      1) Statutory language
      2) Precedents
      3) Policy

1) The plain meaning of the statute requires actual entry into the building. Even the definition urged by the state recognizes that an actual intrusion is required. The language simply cannot be stretched to include activities outside the building.

2) Even if the language of the statute was not conclusive, <u>King</u> would not compel a different result. In <u>King</u>, the defendant cut a hole in a security gate that enclosed a vestibule area. As the court recognized, the vestibule was functionally equivalent to a display window. By fencing the area off, the shopkeeper had incorporated it into the building as much as if it were enclosed by glass.

      While it might be good policy to include "climbing onto a building with the intent to commit a crime" in the burglary statute, the legislature has not

59

done so. It is not the province of the court to alter the statute (institutional competence argument).

Furthermore, it is not clear that any policy would be served by allowing the defendant to be prosecuted for burglary, since there are other criminal statutes which need not be stretched to apply to his conduct (trespass, attempted arson, etc.).

Exercise 11-B: Answers

This exercise provides another broad range of arguments to use in analyzing a different entrapment issue: who is an "agent" of a public officer or employee.

1.   The types of materials.

a.   Statutory, including the language of the statute itself, legislative history materials, related Illinois statutes, and similar statutes in other states.

b.   Case precedents first from Illinois courts, then from other jurisdictions.

c.   Secondary materials, including hornbooks, law review articles, A.L.R. annotations, and dictionary definitions.

d.   Law enforcement agency regulations and agency policies.

2.   This question can be the basis of a class discussion. You can draw on the types of analyses in this chapter, including Part 3 of this exercise.

3.   Identifying types of Arguments

Statutory Arguments

a.   This is a portion of the legislative history, and is the only legislative history available for a fairly old state statute. The commentary seems to favor the interpretation that an agent need not know she is acting on behalf of the police ("the defense has been recognized . . . when [the person] was an investigator privately hired and acting without contact with law enforcement authorities"), but the only case provided is off point and decided on the basis of consent, not entrapment.

b.   This is an argument from statutory language, or lack of it. The writer is using a familiar statutory argument: if the legislature meant to require a knowing agent, it knew how to say so because it did say so in another section. Thus it would have said so here. The example of the legislature "knowing how to say so" is a little off point, however. The example refers to a section from the general part of a criminal code about the mens rea requirement of a criminal offense. Entrapment, however, is a defense to a crime. If the section referred to were related to an entrapment defense, this argument would be stronger.

g.   This argument is a variant of the one above but without the reference to a specific section. If the legislature intended a particular interpretation, it would have said so. The legislature cannot be assumed to have envisioned all these issues at the time the bill was passed, however, and this argument would not be dispositive. If the legislature approved of police using unknowing intermediaries, it may also have said so.

i.   This is another argument from what the legislature did not do, and a variant of "the legislature knew how to define when it wanted to." However, the argument can also lead to the conclusion that the legislature intended to restrict the term agent to its "plain" or dictionary meaning (in "j" below), or it may also mean that the legislature never thought about defining the term.

j. Black's dictionary may be used to supply a "plain meaning" of the statutory term. The definition suggests that an agent knows that she acts for a principal.

Case Analysis

c. Common law argument based on conflicting lines of authority: The analysis of these cases will be among the most important of the parties' arguments. The cases can be reconciled by their factual distinctions. The closer case to the problem in this exercise is the second case described, where the private party did not initiate the contact with the police officer, but served only as an unknowing go-between to the defendant. Because the police initiated the relationship, they were more involved and the court instructed on entrapment.

d. Common law argument based on conflicting lines of authority: Analysis of these cases shows that nationally the issue has not been resolved and there should be valid arguments on either side. The students would have to read these federal cases for their reasoning and their factual patterns. If the decisions align similarly with the Illinois appellate cases based on their facts, then the difference in the private party's role is analytically an important one.

f. Common law argument: broad and narrow interpretation. This case analysis also singles out an important factor: police instruct the private party to target the particular defendant, thus initiating the defendant's entrapment. The student then has to make the factual analogy to the problem in the exercise that describing the defendant without naming him is the same for these purposes as naming him.

Policy Analysis

e. This raises normative arguments about the potential consequences of a rule that permits police to use unknowing private parties and avoid an entrapment instruction: police will increasingly use the unknowing party as a middleman, and perhaps this will become a standard police practice. However, if the middleman is herself entrapped into a criminal act and avails herself of an entrapment instruction, then a new issue is whether the targeted defendant is also entitled to the instruction. (This is called "vicarious entrapment.")

h. This is a "judicial administration" type of argument; the law enforcement agencies can best control abuses by using their own guidelines and can best "police" themselves. Some people may prefer this allocation of authority over court enforcement of a rule that permits an entrapment instruction when police use an unknowing party, because under the court's rule the criminal defendant will go free.

k. This is a normative argument about the consequences of a rule. The rule that the defendant is permitted an entrapment instruction presents a moral hazard: it will result in collusion between the defendant and the middleman and in their perjury.

Note: The Illinois court decided the agency issue using other language in the statute. The court required evidence that the agent himself induced the offense "for the purpose of obtaining evidence for the prosecution" of the defendant. Since an unknowing agent most likely would not know of a contemplated prosecution, this evidence would not be available. <u>People v. Wielgos</u>, 587 N.E.2d 1023 (Ill. 1992).

Exercise 11-C: Answers

1. a) This is an argument from the plain meaning of the statutory language, for Mr. Mack.

b) This is a social goal, policy argument for Ms. Mack.

c) This is an argument from legislative history, which can be interpreted for either party. An interpretation for Ms. Mack is that Congress intended the law to apply to lawyers because they are "like" law enforcement personnel. An interpretation for Mr. Mack is that Congress knew that spouses used wiretapping against each other and still used the language "any person."

2. The first interpretation is the best. Why else would the language have been changed? If "may" had been the original language, one could argue that it was ambiguous. But the legislature must have intended the change from "shall" to "may" to have meaning. Moreover, Congress distinguished "shall assess," which it retained in § 2500(c)(1), and "may assess" in § 2520.

However, one court interpreted the language as mandatory. If that decision were binding or from a particularly important court, it would support that interpretation.

3. At least two federal courts have held that a custodial parent's tap of a minor child's telephone conversations does not come within the Act. Their reasons were that the parent needs to obtain information about the child's welfare, and Congress would not have intended to decide questions of family privacy within the home. The courts broadly interpret Section 2510(5)(a)(i), which exempts interceptions by phone extensions used by a "user in the ordinary course of business," to apply to home phones as well as to commercial phones. See Scheib v. Grant, 22 F.3d 149 (7th Cir. 1994); Newcomb v. Ingle, 944 F.2d 1534 (10th Cir. 1991).

Chapter Twelve

Research Strategies

This chapter is an overview of the legal research process in which we relate this process to the students' legal analysis and writing. This chapter does not teach basic legal bibliography, and we do not include basic information about using legal research books. We do emphasize to students that there is a logic behind the legal research process and point out strategies that they may use. The type of problem they are working on, the information with which they begin, the materials that are available, and the costs involved will determine the paths that students' research should take. The chapter would be appropriate to assign after the students have done at least one research memorandum. Alternatively, you may want to assign the chapter before your students begin their first research memo assignment, just after they have learned the basic bibliographic information.

We have attempted to take students through a research project, based on various alternatives. We have used the familiar classification of research materials as primary authorities, secondary authorities, and search materials. We begin with determining the claim or defense involved in the problem. The first research alternative is for the student (or attorney) who already knows some citations to relevant materials and wants to expand the search. The other alternative is for the student who begins with no citations. In this latter context, we discuss indexing methods and problems of indexing. We also briefly discuss particular research problems, such as federal statutory issues.

In this edition, we have expanded our discussion of using technology as part of a research strategy. Now, students should not only be proficient in using books and computer-assisted legal research (CALR); they should also know that CD-ROM services and the Internet are increasingly important in doing research. More and more law offices are replacing books with CD-ROM services because of the savings in space, convenience, and even money. Some lawyers now talk about the paperless or virtual office, as lawyers use technology to rationalize their case files, to communicate with each other, and to browse legal research databases. Moreover, LEXIS and WESTLAW now offer financial packages for limited sources that make CALR more affordable for small firms and even solo practitioners. And the Internet can provide free access to some materials (cases from the federal circuit courts and the state supreme courts), rapid access to other materials that previously would have been difficult to obtain (new federal agency rulings), and access to a wide range of nonlegal materials. So the question is no longer whether to use books or computers, but when to use them.

A law graduate must be familiar with all of the available legal research sources: books, CALR, CD-ROM, and the Internet.

Exercise 12-A, p. 212: Answers

These exercises are designed to give students examples of different kinds of research problems and to show how they require different approaches and different research tools. The following suggested answers are given as of April 1999. The law may change, so specific answers may need to be changed too.

1.   This is an example of a research problem in which computers are particularly useful. The case will not be available in the hard-copy (e.g., U.S.L.W.) for a week or so. To find the case on the computer, first select the appropriate database or library file--SCT or US (cases decided by the Supreme Court of the United States.) Then do a field search (WESTLAW) or segment search (LEXIS) using the parties' last names. You could also add the date of the opinion. On WESTLAW the search would be: title(Faragher & Boca) and da(is 6/26/98); in LEXIS the search would be: name (Faragher & Boca) and date is 6/26/98.

2.   This is a complex problem requiring research on a number of levels. Since the term "sexual harassment" in CALR would yield hundreds of cases, the better way to proceed would be to get a more complete understanding of the facts and then to get background material. The students will probably know that sexual harassment is a form of sex discrimination. However, they may not know that a party can be liable for sexual harassment under federal law, under most state laws, and under some municipal laws.

A)   Federal law prohibits discrimination in employment, including sex discrimination under Title VII of the Civil Rights Act of 1964, as amended, 42 U.S.C. §2000e et seq. (1994). You could begin by looking up the term "sexual harassment" in the Index to the U.S. Code Annotated. The references in the Index are quite lengthy (though they do refer you to different sections of the employment discrimination statute.) Since this is a theory under which hundreds of cases have been brought, rather than going directly to the Index to the U.S. Code Annotated, the more practical way to begin would be to get background information by looking either to a treatise in employment discrimination (i.e., Charles A. Sullivan, Michael J. Zimmer, and Richard F. Richards, Employment Discrimination (2d ed. 1988) or to the Index to Legal Periodicals or the Current Law Index for law review articles. Since the alleged harassment took place in Philadelphia, which is in the Third Circuit, the binding law would come from the

United States Supreme Court and the Third Circuit. As the office has 35 employees (more than 15), the office would be considered an "employer" within the meaning of Title VII.

To find any recent Supreme Court decisions, a good place to look is United States Law Week, Supreme Court edition. The index to the 1998-99 term yields four Supreme Court cases. These cases summarize the only other two Supreme Court cases dealing with sexual harassment and elaborate on the viability of same-sex harassment and the nature of the employer's liability. To find cases in the Third Circuit, you could update using a citator the two Supreme Court cases, looking only for cases in the Third Circuit; you could note Third Circuit cases identified in the treatises and law review articles; you could check a looseleaf service, like Employment Practices Decisions for cases. You could also try CALR, formulating a search using terms from the facts and limiting the search to cases from the Third Circuit. Finally, you would make note of cases with similar facts decided in other circuits, which would be persuasive.

The agency charged with the administration of Title VII, the Equal Employment Opportunity Commission, has promulgated regulations dealing with sexual harassment. The important sections will be noted in the cases, but they can be found independently through a search of C.F.R.

B) Many states have laws that prohibit sex discrimination. Therefore, Ms. Abbott's rights may also have been violated under the Pennsylvania anti-discrimination statute. Since this search is limited to the law of one state, a good place to start is the index to the Pennsylvania Code Annotated. Try terms like "discrimination," "sex discrimination," "sexual harassment" and "labor and employment." They will lead you to 43 Pa. Stat. Ann §955 et seq. You would then look up the statute and read it. The term "sexual harassment" does not appear in the statute. But you can look in the Notes of Decisions to find cases interpreting the statute. Note 18.5, on the topic of hostile work environment, collects sexual harassment cases. Another way of finding cases that interpret the statute is to update the statute.

It is less likely that there are law review articles dealing with state law on this question, but there may be. Also, some states have their own legal encyclopedias, which may be helpful.

The same process could be followed to research the code on the computer by formulating a query, but there is not much advantage in using material that is exactly the same as that in the book when a book is easier to read than a screen.

C)   Finally, the city of Philadelphia may have an anti-discrimination ordinance which prohibits sex discrimination, including sexual harassment. To find this, look in the municipal code. If there are no case annotations, check the state digest.

3.   You have some basic information in that you know the federal statute under which your client has been charged. But like the Title VII statute in exercise 2, the federal murder statute has been interpreted in hundreds or even thousands of cases. The first step is to read the second degree murder statute itself. But then a next useful step would be to read a criminal law treatise to get a general idea of defenses based on the mental condition of the defendant. Treatises will include both state and federal cases in the footnotes and will provide a starting point.

There are different ways to proceed from here. One is to look up law review articles that deal with Post Traumatic Stress Disorder. This may also be referred to as Vietnam Stress Syndrome. These articles will probably refer to federal cases in which the defendant has attempted to use the mental disorder as a defense to a crime.

To see if there is an insanity defense under federal law, the place to look is the United States Code. Using the print copy rather than the computer works well here. If you look in the Index to the U.S.C.A. under "insanity," you will find a reference to the Insanity Defense Reform Act, 18 U.S.C. §17 (1994). (Looking up the phrase "mental illness" does not work very well.) The statute is short and the annotations contain some very useful cases. Most of the relevant cases can be found this way; others can be found because they are cited in these cases or through updating using a citator. These cases refer both to the insanity defense itself, and also to the question of mental illness as a means of negating an element of the crime, like intent. There are also a number of law review articles on the insanity defense which you can find through the Index to Legal Periodicals or the Current Law Index.

4.   This is another case in which computers are particularly useful. In fact, it would be very difficult to get this information any other way. You would first get the database for the relevant Supreme Court Justice. And then you would do a search using terms like "confront!/5 clause".

Chapter Thirteen

Interviewing the Client

The chapters on Interviewing and Counseling, and the material in Chapter Fifteen on writing client letters are related. Even if you decide not to assign Exercise 13-A in which the students are asked to conduct an interview and write a Memo to the File, you will probably want to assign Chapter Thirteen as background reading if you are assigning Chapter Fourteen or Fifteen. The students will benefit from reading the material in Chapter Thirteen on the lawyer/client relationship when they do any assignments relating to client counseling, either at an in-personal meeting or by letter.

In this chapter "Interviewing the Client," and the following chapter, "Counseling the Client," we are not trying to teach students the skills of interviewing and counseling. These are complex skills and ones that we hope the students will begin to develop in their upper-class clinics and courses. However, even in the first year, it is important for students to understand that their relationship with the client is not limited to their getting the facts and then deciding what legal advice to give. And their writing will benefit from their having a clearer sense of the actual context in which the client's legal questions arise.

Our approach is that of client-centered counseling, discussed fully in such texts as David Binder *et al.*, Lawyers as Counselors: A Client-Centered Approach (1991) and Joseph Bastress *et al.*, Interviewing, Counseling and Negotiation: Skills for Effective Representation (1990). Students may be surprised to learn that in their relationship with the client, the legal question is not the only question, and sometimes not even the most important question. They may be surprised to realize that their interpersonal skills may be as important as their analytic skills, and that listening is as important as talking. They may be surprised to know that they need to be aware of the Model Rules of Professional Conduct in their dealings with the client. Finally, they may be surprised to discover that despite their years in law school, the client is the ultimate decision-maker.

One hypothetical [introduced in Exercise 6-A(3)] is used both in this chapter and Chapter Fourteen on counseling. The hypothetical concerns a client, John Starr, who has come to the lawyer because of his desire to get some sort of satisfaction from the Pennsylvania Deluxe Hotel, an entity he holds indirectly responsible for his wife's injury. Mr. Starr's case is the basis for the sections on preparation for the interview, the interview itself, and the Memo to the File. In Chapter Fourteen, the students will be asked to write a counseling plan for a meeting with Mr. Starr and to actually conduct the counseling meeting.

We also introduce the students to a different kind of writing in this chapter, the lawyer's Memo to the File, giving as an example the memo written in Mr. Starr's case.   The text provides the suggested content for a memo. However, these memos will undoubtedly vary in form and content from office to office and case to case.

Exercise 13-A

This exercise combines the lawyering exercise of a client interview with the writing assignment of writing a Memo to the File. We did not want to provide the text of an interview in the book and then have the students write a Memo to the File based on the interview. Their Memos would likely restate the text of the interview without much insight either in eliciting facts, understanding the client's objectives and feelings, or establishing a rapport with the client. Instead, we suggest that you have the students conduct an interview. You could play the role of the client, Anne Atkins, or have a student in the class, a former student, or a research assistant play that role. Note: You could expand this exercise by having the students actually research the legal question. The significant cases can be found in the West Group Digest under the topic False Imprisonment, key numbers 1-5.

I.   Planning the Interview

It is important to give the students time to prepare for the interview. Otherwise you would be encouraging the idea that they can just wing it. So you could assign the students Exercise 13-A and give them a few days or a week to write a plan for the interview. You could either have all of the students in the class act as the lawyer, ask for volunteers, or assign one or two students to do the interview on the day of the interview class.

The students' written plan could include:

-the content of the interview
-the interview's structure
-the questions they would need to ask to determine Ms. Atkins
objectives and the facts of her case
-any problems they foresee.

II.   The Legal Standard

Ms. Atkins might have a legal claim based on false imprisonment. There are three requirements for false imprisonment. [For more information on the tort of false imprisonment, see Chapters Four and Five.]

Basically, an actor is liable for false imprisonment if

1. he acts intending to confine the other or a third person within boundaries fixed by the actor;
2. his act directly or indirectly results in such confinement (Confinement may be brought about by actual physical barriers, by submission to physical force, or by threats of physical force.); and
3. the other is conscious of the confinement or is harmed by it.

Anne would be arguing confinement by threat of physical force.

III. The Facts of Anne Atkins' Case

Anne is 23-years old. She lived at home until September, 1997, when she got a job as a buyer in a department store, became self-supporting, and moved into her own apartment. Eight months ago Anne's friend, Joyce Brown, suggested that Anne come with her to a discussion group and communal dinner sponsored by the Family of Truth and Light, an organization to which Joyce belonged. Anne attended the discussion and dinner and was greatly impressed by the warmth and dedication of the people she met, and the insight of the group leader. She began to attend the nightly meetings of the group and, every weekend, to visit the collective farm run by members of the Family. At this farm, members of the Family participated in a number of activities that generated revenue to support the Family -- raising chickens, vegetables, and house plants, making candles, and running a restaurant.

Anne said she grew to feel closer to the members of the Family than she did to her own parents, with whom she had always had a rather remote relationship with her (although she was quite close to her younger brother, Barry).

Last month Anne decided to become a member of the Family of Truth and Light and to live on its collective farm. She called her parents on the telephone to tell them. They were angry and upset. They said that she was making a terrible mistake, that members of the Family were a bunch of crazy kooks and misfits with a weird religion, and that they (her parents) would not let her ruin her life. Anne told them she had made up her mind and would come to the house at 6 p.m. on Monday night, a week later, to pick up some of her books and personal items.

That Monday night Anne arrived at her parents' house. After Anne came in, her mother told Barry to leave them alone and to go out and visit a friend. He protested but finally did as he was told. Anne went up to the room that had been hers to collect her things.

A few minutes later the doorbell rang. Anne then heard people coming up the stairs. She heard her father say, "I appreciate your help, Barton," and a stranger's voice replying, "You won't regret it." Her parents entered the room along with a man Anne had never seen before. She estimated he was about 6'2" and weighed about 225 pounds. (Anne is 5'2" and weighs 115 pounds.) Her parents closed the door. They told her not to go and live on the Family's collective farm. They said they loved her very much and only wanted what was best for her. Anne's mother began to cry and said she would never forgive herself if Anne joined the Family. She said they had given Anne everything when she was a child. Anne said that she did not want to discuss it with them, that she was not a child any longer (the age of majority in this state is 18), and that she just wanted to get her things and leave.

Anne's father then said that they should all go on a vacation together and that all she needed to get the Family nonsense out of her system was to get away for a while. Her father continued pressing her to agree to the vacation and Anne kept saying that she did not want to discuss her decision with them and she just wanted to leave. While all of this was going on, the large man who had accompanied her parents just stood there with his arms folded over his chest. Occasionally the man would nod when her father said something. Anne had not paid much attention to him at first, but after a few minutes, her father referred to him again as "Barton." Anne remembered from her discussions with people in the Family that two former members had been kidnapped by a Jim Barton at the request of their parents, and that Barton had "deprogrammed" them. Anne had heard that his methods were not only psychological, but also violent. She became more and more frightened as her parents continued to urge her not to join the Family. After four hours in the room with her parents and Barton, Anne finally agreed that she would not join the Family and would stop attending its meetings.

IV. Other Issues

There are other issues you should raise in the interview as well. Anne is very resentful of her parents' continuous efforts to run her life. She is referring not only to the incident with Barton, but her whole life before that. She feels that her parents were always pushing her to do things that she didn't want to do, making decisions for her, treating her like a child, and imposing their values on her. She is both furious at them and concerned about whether they will ever talk to her again if she sues them. (Quite appropriately.) She is worried about cutting her ties completely and wonders if she could sue Barton, but not her parents.

She is also concerned about the impact of an award of damages on her parents' financial situation, particularly because her mother has just been downsized from her long-time job and is unsure that she can find a comparable position. Anne does not want to drive her parents into bankruptcy.

Finally, Anne is beginning to have second thoughts about the Family of Truth and Light. At this point, Anne still goes to some evening meetings and spends some weekends there, but she no longer wishes to live on the commune.

Chapter Fourteen

Counseling the Client

Chapter Fourteen focuses on the process of client decision-making, again adopting the client-centered approach. It also introduces the students to another example of lawyer's writing, the counseling plan. Our goal is to encourage students to prepare carefully for a counseling meeting with a client. The final exercise has the students simulate a counseling meeting.

You should assign as reading Chapter Thirteen as well as Chapter Fourteen, even if you do not intend to give the students exercises from Chapter Thirteen. Much of the detail on the lawyer's relationship to the client and the process of listening to and questioning the client appears in the Chapter Thirteen on interviewing. Students who have not read it will have less understanding of how to conduct a counseling meeting.

Exercise 14-A

In this exercise, the students are asked to complete the counseling plan for John Starr's counseling meeting.

Option #2 - Bring a lawsuit

Pros
-John feels strongly that the hotel should pay for his suffering and the dislocation to his life, his wife's, and his aunt's
-He may get financial compensation from hotel in damages
-He could expose hotel's carelessness

Cons
-strain on marriage will continue and maybe get worse
-cost of litigation
-time litigation could take to resolve the issue
-uncertainty in strength of legal claim because did not view shooting directly, and because has no physical symptoms
-weakness in claim if Jane is hostile or even neutral, since she would be one of the main witnesses

-Alice wants nothing more to do with it. Will she have to be called as a witness?

Questions to John

How strongly does Jane feel against bringing this lawsuit? Will she refuse to cooperate? How will the suit affect their marriage?

Will Alice likely continue her refusal to talk about the situation? How would John then deal with her involvement in the incident?

Does he realize how long the lawsuit may take and the financial resources the hotel has in defending this case?

Is this the only way in which he feels he can put an end to the incident?

Option # 3- Try to negotiate a settlement with the hotel. Write a letter as his lawyer and see response.

Pros
-less stressful to marriage because less confrontational on John's part
-possibility of quick resolution
-no need to bother Alice
-does not point out Jane's ambivalence
-if hotel stonewalls, he can consider suing

Cons
-no guarantee they will respond affirmatively
-much smaller money damages

Questions for John

How important is it to him that the hotel admit its responsibility, since it will refuse to admit liability as a condition of settlement? Does he think Jane will find this route more acceptable?

Is he prepared to accept much less in damages?

Exercise 14-B

This exercise is the culmination of Mr. Starr's case. Ideally, all of the students have completed exercise 14-A and have written a counseling plan for the meeting with John Starr. Even if you decide not to assign 14-A, however, you can still assign Exercise 14-B to the class. In either case, the students will need a few days to prepare.

The students can conduct the exercise out of class, or in class, if you have a large enough room for the students to be able to conduct the meeting without disturbing each other.

Divide the class, with half of the students playing the role of John Starr and half playing the role of the lawyer. Assign pairs ahead of time, each with one lawyer and one client. Have the students conduct a counseling meeting of approximately 20-30 minutes, and then bring the class together to reflect on their experience.

You might want to ask the lawyers what options they had included in their plan, what questions they felt they needed to ask to try to and help Mr. Starr see the pros and cons of the options, whether they were able to get a sense of Mr. Starr's priorities, and how they planned on responding if Mr. Starr asked them what he should do.

You might want to ask the clients whether they thought the lawyer had prepared carefully for the meeting, whether the lawyer listened to their concerns, whether the lawyer was trying to impose a decision on them, and whether they felt confidence in the lawyer.

Chapter Fifteen

Letter Writing

Before turning to the letter exercises at the end of this chapter, you may want to have some classroom discussion of the sample letters in the chapter. If you haven't assigned the chapters on interviewing and counseling, you may want to talk about the lawyer's role in counseling. Many students may think it is part of their job to tell their clients what their wisest course of action is. You may need to explain why this is not always the best course of action. Chapters Thirteen and Fourteen in the text and the manual go into this in some detail.

You might want to draw students' attention to the roadmap paragraph that opens the legal analysis section and stress the importance of this paragraph in orienting the reader. You could also discuss whether headings would be appropriate in this letter.

It might be useful to compare the fact statements in the letter to Park Crest Hospital and the letter to Mr. Braun. Note where and why the facts differ. Compare the two analyses. Is it appropriate to cite cases in the adversary letter and not in the client letter? Why or why not? Discuss the tone of the adversary letter. Some students might find it more conciliatory than they expected. Is it justified?

Finally, discuss the letter to the third party. We ourselves were conflicted on whether to raise the subpoena in this letter. Perhaps it would make more sense to raise it only if the first letter fails. What rhetorical techniques does the writer use to persuade Ms. Wells to testify?

Exercise 15-B(1) involves a lot of background reading. You could assign it as homework. The students' critiques could then be the bases for the rewriting exercise, which could be done in small groups in class. Alternatively, the students could read the materials at home, but do the critique in class. Exercises 15-A and 15-B(2) can be done either in class or at home. Exercise 15-C is a counseling exercise. You could do it either before or after the Letter Writing exercise in 15-B, depending on whether you want the letter to prepare the client for your meeting or to help your client reflect on your meeting.

Exercise 15-A: Answers

1.   (a) The opening sentence is patronizing and unnecessarily negative given the fact that courts assess mental injuries routinely. The writer needs to go on to state the law in terms comprehensible to a lay client and to name the options, *i.e.*, more content is needed.

        (b) The first sentence contains a dangling modifier and is both wordy and overly certain. It is not clear if a court would find the client's reasons for suing are without question meritorious, nor is it appropriate to judge the client's motives for suing.
        From this overly certain tone, the writer moves to an unnecessarily uncertain tone. Instead of stressing that anything could happen were the case to go to court, the writer should give more of a legal assessment.
        The options are set out, but the writer should consider more carefully the impact of stating an opinion so early in the letter and in the process. Will the client be overly influenced? Is the advice premature since the client has not yet expressed his own opinions on the options?
        An adequate roapmap of the letter's organization is provided.

        (c) The opening is vague and somewhat peremptory. The writer should state the issue to be discussed. The second sentence doesn't make it clear that the purpose of the letter is to provide an explanation of the law. The tone is dictatorial rather than courteous.

2.   The law is accurately stated in the first paragraph. The writer could perhaps personalize it by couching the elements in terms of what the client must show: "we have to prove that you were closely related to the victim...etc."
        The writer may be overly optimistic about establishing the first three elements. In particular, there should be some discussion of how severe an injury need be when there is no physical injury. In addition, the writer's suggestion that the client stay home is cynical and unethical, as well as insensitive to the impact this advice might have on the client's finances and emotional well being.
        The writer may be overly negative about establishing the last element. In addition, the discussion may mystify the client, who may not understand the bearing *Trask v. Vincent* has on his case. Moreover, the summary of that case and the ensuing analogy are callously written, ignoring the trauma the client has undergone.

3.   The writer needs to exhibit more tact in discussing the non-legal issues. The grim picture the writer paints of the family's reaction to litigation, coupled with a gloomy prognosis of the outcome of litigation, may unfairly promote the

option the lawyer favors.

In addition, the writer is too quick to suggest concessions the client should make. Does the client really want to pursue settlement talks, for which he would be incurring legal fees, but may receive no damages? Has the writer made a decision about the client's motives and desires precipitously? It would probably be a better idea to ask the client what would satisfy him.

Although the writer reassures the client that the decision is his, the reassurance is not convincing given the context. Perhaps some of the pros of litigation needed to be spelled out.

Exercise 15-B: Answers

1.   Reproduced below is the advice letter to Mr. Eliot with marginal comments suggesting some of its problems.

———

Dear Mr. Eliot,

Refer to the 2 questions Eliot raised   This letter gives you my opinion of how a New York court would rule on the restrictive covenant contained in your prospective employment contract at this moment in time. I cannot guarantee the court will agree with my analysis. In

wordy
Also too defensive { addition, the law upon which I am basing my analysis is always subject to change by the courts or possibly the legislature. Furthermore, I have written this letter for your benefit only and not for the benefit of third parties. The letter is not to be used for any purpose other than for your information. Finally, I have based

Does this rote incantation pertain to this problem? Are the facts in question here? Also include a roadmap { my opinion in part on the facts that you gave me at our meeting. If you misstated them then, or have since remembered facts, please let me know since a change in facts might change my analysis.

Set out factors — Then take one-by-one   In determining whether a covenant not to compete is reasonable, courts examine a number of factors. First, an employer has a legitimate interest in enforcing a restrictive covenant not to compete in order to protect himself from unfair competition resulting from the loss of an employee's unique services. Although an employee's extraordinary services can be

Wordy { justification for the enforceability of a covenant not to compete, enforcement usually is not granted merely on the basis of the

78

uniqueness of the employee's services. Reasonable time and geographic restrictions must be set forth in a covenant in order for it to be enforceable. In Quandt, a covenant not to compete that contained reasonable time and territory limitations was not enforced because the salesperson's duties were not extraordinary in nature. The services of an employee who acts merely in the capacity of an effective and well-trained salesperson may be valuable but are not so unique that their loss would result in irreparable damage or unfair competition to the employer. Quandt's Wholesale Distributors v. Giardino, 448 N.Y.S.2d 809, 810 (App. Div. 1982). In fact, in Quandt, the sales in the employee's territory were equal if not greater once he terminated his employment.

The salesperson being hired by Toydyno will be expected to solicit new customers to promote the Knobots. However, this is not an extraordinary job requirement that any salesperson would not be expected or able to fulfill. The anticipated duties of this salesperson are not so unique that performance by another individual would cause Toydyno to incur a loss.

Although an employee's skills may not be classified as unique, a restrictive covenant may be enforced in order to prevent the use or disclosure of confidential customer information or trade secrets. It is highly likely that the "source codes" and the technique for making "flange-hinges" would be considered trade secrets. Not only is this information highly technical and probably the result of long hours of costly research, but it is so intrinsically related to the manufacture of the Knobot that its exploitation would cause Toydyno considerable harm. Therefore, it is likely that a court would uphold the provision of the covenant that prohibits you from disclosing this information.

The customer lists that you will be privy to may also be construed as confidential since they will contain business information that might give you an unfair competitive advantage. In Scott Paper Co. v. Finnegan, 476 N.Y.S.2d 316 (App. Div. 1984), a regional sales manager employed by a paper manufacturer signed a restrictive covenant prohibiting him from using business information including customer preference data, pricing and promotional information, customer buying records and other business information. When he left his employer and

79

began working for another paper company, his former employer attempted to enjoin him from using this information. The court, however, held that it was either readily available from other sources like distributors in the paper industry, or, as was the case with the pricing information, no longer relevant.

It is not clear if the business information on the client lists that you will have possession of would be obtainable from different sources. Assuming that it would not be—particularly the credit information—it is possible that you could gain an unfair advantage were you to use it. Hence, the information will most probably be deemed confidential and you will not be able to keep the lists.

Even though you will not be able to keep the lists, you will be able to maintain your customer contacts. The test applied by the courts in deciding when the identity of a customer is confidential is whether the customer's name is readily obtainable from an outside source. <u>Columbia Ribbon v. A-1-A Corp.</u>, 369 N.E.2d 4 (N.Y. 1977). The customer contacts you will make will not be confidential. Your customers will include camera stores, bookstores, and sporting goods stores. Since the identity of these customers can be obtained in any business directory, a court would not consider them trade secrets. For the same reason, your original contacts in department stores in the region could not be construed as confidential either.

There is also the issue of the reasonableness of time and geographic restrictions. Here courts examine their scope and duration as well as a showing of unfair competition. If you were to use or disclose the business information on the customer lists, it would be reasonable only to enjoin you from competing in the area where that information would be relevant. It should be noted, however, that no geographical limitation could prevent you from selling electronic toys or anything else absent your possession and utilization of a trade secret or confidential customer lists.

To sum up, since Toydyno's "computer source codes," and the technique for making "flange-hinges" are trade secrets, the court may prevent you from disclosing or using them. Although you may have to return the customer lists because they *time and geographic restrictions?* contain confidential business information, you will be able to maintain your customer contacts since they are readily obtainable from other sources. Thus, you will be able to compete with Toydyno as long as you do not use any trade secrets or confidential information.

governing? *refresh reader's memory* *phrase more tactfully* *Explain.* *other option* *Wait! Ask for instructions* Ultimately, therefore, you should agree to clauses 1(c) and 2. Not only is Toydyno within its rights in demanding this information be kept confidential, but in all frankness, your employment prospects are not so bright that you can flatly reject all restrictions. However, you should not agree to 1(a) and (b), at least in their present form. I will write to Toydyno proposing these terms. Please call me if you have any questions.

Very truly yours,

2. Below we include a possible rewrite of the attorney's letter to Mr. Eliot.

_____

81

101 Park Avenue
New York, New York 10178
June 16, _____

Mr. Timothy S. Eliot
234 Main Street
Larchmont, New York 07090

Re: Toydyno's Restrictive Covenant

Dear Mr. Eliot,

During our conversation last week, you asked me to research whether Toydyno will be able to enforce the restrictive covenant contained in your prospective employment contract and whether any of the provisions of that contract should be negotiated.

Generally, courts frown upon post-employment restrictive covenants and subject them to a strict standard of reasonableness because they are not eager to deprive a person of a livelihood. Thus, covenants not to compete are enforced only when an employee's services are unique or extraordinary or when they prevent the disclosure or use of confidential customer lists or trade secrets. Additionally, they must be reasonable in temporal and geographical scope.

Toydyno's restrictive covenant is too broad geographically and temporally to be enforced in New York. Although I would not at this time demand that these terms be redrafted, you might want to informally request Toydyno to propose an area and time limit that is equitable to both parties. I have set out below my reasoning on these issues and urge you to consider my analysis carefully.

Unique Service Provisions

In determining whether a covenant not to compete is reasonable, courts examine a number of factors. First, an employer has a legitimate interest in enforcing a covenant not to compete in order to protect against unfair competition resulting from the loss of an employee's unique services. In the past, courts have deemed the services of an employee who acts merely in the capacity of an effective and well-trained salesperson as valuable, but not so unique that his or her loss would result in irreparable damage or unfair competition to the employer.

The salesperson being hired by Toydyno will be expected to solicit new customers to promote the Knobots. However, this is not an extraordinary job requirement that any salesperson would not be expected or able to fulfill. The anticipated duties of this salesperson are not so unique that performance by another individual would cause Toydyno to incur a loss.

Customer Lists and Trade Secret Provisions

Although an employee's skills may not be classified as unique, a restrictive covenant may be enforced in order to prevent the use or disclosure of confidential customer information or trade secrets. Information on the unique technology or manufacturing process of a product is a trade secret. It is highly likely that the "source codes" and the technique for making "flange-hinges" would be considered trade secrets. Not only is this information highly technical and probably the result of long hours of costly research, but it is so intrinsically related to the manufacture of the Knobot that its exploitation would cause Toydyno considerable harm. Therefore, it is likely that a court would uphold the provision of the covenant that prohibits you from disclosing this information.

The customer lists that you will be privy to may also be construed as confidential since they will contain business information that might give you an unfair competitive advantage. Courts have upheld provisions prohibiting the use of business information--including customer preference data, pricing and promotional information, and customer buying records. It is not clear if the business information on the client lists that you will have possession of would be obtainable from different sources. Assuming that it would not be—particularly the credit information—it is possible that you could gain an unfair advantage were you to use it. Hence, the information may be deemed confidential and you would not be able to keep the lists.

Even though you may not be able to keep the lists, you will be able to maintain your customer contacts. The test applied by the courts in deciding when the identity of a customer is confidential is whether the customer's name is readily obtainable from an outside source. The customer contacts you will make will not be confidential. Your customers will include camera stores, bookstores, and sporting goods stores. Since the identity of these customers can be obtained in any business directory, a court would not consider them trade secrets. For the same reason, your original contacts in department stores in the region could not be construed as confidential either.

Geography and Time Provisions

Even when trade secrets or an employee's extraordinary services justifies enforcing a covenant not to compete, enforcement usually is not granted merely on those bases. Reasonable time and geographic restrictions must be set forth in a covenant in order for it to be enforceable.

Generally, geographic restrictions are limited to sales territory. Courts, ever mindful of competition, will not enforce a no compete clause beyond a firm's territory because that would essentially give the former employer a free and undeserved monopoly and limit the free market in contravention of public policy. Since Toydyno seeks to restrict your activities nationwide, its geographic provision is probably too broad.

Time restrictions are generally upheld if they are limited to a period of six months to two years. A great deal of technological know-how and market data loses its value over time. Customers leave, the market changes, needs change. Thus, two years appears to be the upper limit of temporal restrictiveness; nonetheless, importance of the information you are forbidden to share may effect the time. I am confident, though, that no court would uphold the indefinite period your contract assigns, and would most likely enforce only up to a year, given the ever-changing computer market where ideas that are fresh one day become commonplace the next.

To sum up, since Toydyno's "computer source codes," and the technique for making "flange-hinges" are trade secrets, a court might prevent you from disclosing or using them. Similarly, the customer lists might be protected because they contain confidential business information. You would be able to maintain your customer contacts, however, since they are readily obtainable from other sources. Finally, Toydyno's time and geography restrictions are probably overbroad. Thus, were your relationship with Toydyno to end, you would be able to compete with Toydyno as long as you did not use any trade secrets or confidential information.

Alternatives and Recommendations

On the basis of the analysis above, if you really want the job, you should consider agreeing to clauses 1(c) and 2, which govern confidential customer lists and trade secrets. Not only is Toydyno within its rights in demanding your confidentiality, but the job market is so competitive that even individuals with your experience and expertise are not in a good position to flatly reject all restrictions. However, two clauses are more problematic: 1(a), which governs time and place, and 1(b), which bans the use of even those customer lists that are in the public domain. You have two options here.

While you are certainly within your rights to demand a fair agreement, you may wish to forestall discussion on the particular terms of the restrictive covenant, sign the agreement as is, and wait until an actual issue arises before you challenge the covenant's validity. By demanding new time and geographic provisions when a court would probably nullify them anyway, you may be wasting valuable "negotiation points" on an issue which has been essentially decided in the courts. You may rather decide to negotiate issues which are certainly open (e.g., salary). Moreover, by agreeing to the covenant's terms as is, you will be showing good faith and establishing a strong, congenial relationship with your future employer. In contrast, if you insist that Toydyno entrust a new employee with trade secrets and confidential information (a firm's life's blood) without assurances of confidentiality, you may create bad will, an atmosphere which could effect you when you begin work at Toydyno.

On the other hand, there are good reasons to avoid signing a provision that might need to be litigated. One option might be for me to write Toydyno, explain the situation, and ask, as nicely and as reasonably as possible, if they would consider changing the terms of the restrictions. Perhaps a "soft" letter from an attorney will suggest to Toydyno the benefits of reaching an equitable agreement, one that protects both parties' interests and concerns. If you so instruct me, I will draft a possible letter to Toydyno for your perusal.

You, of course, know Toydyno, know the market, and know yourself. Think about the alternatives available and the various ramifications of those alternatives and let me know how you wish to proceed. I shall call you in a few days to discuss this letter, but in the interim please feel free to contact me directly about any issue that concerns you. I look forward to our conversation.

Very truly yours,

3.   What follows is a sample letter to Toydyno.

———————

101 Park Avenue
New York, New York 10178
June 16, _____

Ms. Rita Baer
Toydyno Industries International
4142 Sixth Avenue
New York, New York 10241

Re: Timothy S. Eliot Restrictive Employment Covenant

Dear Ms. Baer:

I am contacting you concerning the restrictive covenant contained in the employment contract you recently offered Mr. Timothy S. Eliot. Mr. Eliot is very interested in your position, but is worried by the scope and longevity of the covenant's restrictions. Mr. Eliot has a family that he must support and is concerned that such restrictions might damage his ability to provide for them. I offered to write to see if we could tailor the covenant a bit more narrowly and still address your and Mr. Eliot's concerns satisfactorily.

We understand your confidential information must be fully protected. Mr. Eliot does not object to restrictions on computer source codes, the "flange-hinge" trade secret information, the non-public customer lists, and customer purchasing and credit history. The only issue really is the "to anyone anywhere" language. That language effectively forces Mr. Eliot out of a career in which he has invested many years of his life and from which he derives his and his family's livelihood. Moreover, the covenant goes into effect as soon as he leaves you for any reason whatever, including an emergency, a downward market swing, or any number of other essentially innocuous events that have nothing to do with an intent to compete with your firm.

There are two different approaches we could take to protect both you and Mr. Eliot. One would be to limit the time and geography provisions of the agreement to a year and to an area. This way Mr. Eliot could, after a reasonable period of time, provide for his family without competing unfairly with you for customers you have cultivated. Moreover, given the rapid changes in technology and equipment that so define the electronics industry (even the most advanced approaches are rendered obsolete within months of their invention and dissemination), this proposal seems eminently fair and nonthreatening.

Another approach might be to compensate Mr. Eliot for signing the covenant. You could pay him a higher salary, guarantee him a period of employment, make him a cash settlement upon termination, or immediately vest him in the firm's retirement plan. While expensive, this approach could provide Mr. Eliot with the opportunity to train and enter a new field, and also allow you the full restrictive power of the covenant.

Of these two options, I personally favor the first. I tend to think the second alternative is unnecessarily expensive, given that the first offers you adequate protection. However, I believe both these alternatives are equitable and demonstrate our hope that you and Mr. Eliot will have a long and profitable relationship.

If you would like your attorney to speak with me concerning this matter, please have the attorney contact me directly. Otherwise, I shall contact you shortly to arrange a meeting on these matters.

Very truly yours,

Exercise 15-C: Answers

This exercise refers the students back to Exercise 15-B in which they have been asked to edit a letter to Mr. Eliot who has asked his lawyer's advice about a proposed covenant not to compete in an employment contract. For purposes of Exercise 15-C, however, the students will be counseling Mr. Eliot not by letter, but at a meeting in person, the more common method. A personal meeting gives the lawyer an opportunity to make sure the client understands the legal issues and to probe the client's objectives and concerns. The students should begin by planning the counseling meeting.

A lawyer would have little difficulty explaining to Mr. Eliot, an experienced salesman, the concept of a covenant not to compete and the reasons employers seek them. Mr. Eliot can understand the employer's desire to protect itself against losses because of competition from an employee whose services are unique or to prevent the disclosure or use of confidential customer lists or trade secrets. He can also understand that an employer's rights to protect itself are not unlimited and that employers may go too far in demanding concessions by an employee.

Toydyno's proposed covenant has both reasonable and unreasonable aspects. It is unlikely that Mr. Eliot's services would be characterized as unique, as he would be performing the job an ordinarily competent salesman. However, a court would probably characterize Toydyno's "computer source codes" and the technique for making "flange-hinges" as trade secrets appropriate for protection. In addition, because of the detailed information in the customer lists which goes beyond mere names and addresses, a court may protect those as well. However, Toydyno has restricted the use of this information in a way that is unreasonable. Courts will not likely enforce provisions that are unlimited as to time and geography.

Objectives: Mr. Eliot's objectives are probably typical of most potential employees: he wants the job and on the best terms available. Mr. Eliot has had a successful 10-year relationship with current employer, Kid-Vid, but is concerned about the company's continued financial viability, so he is looking for a new job. He is aware that finding a new job will be difficult, particularly at his age and level of experience. As he is "set in his ways," he wants a job that will take advantage of his experience in the field and his methods. Moreover, he wants a salary that is consistent with his prior salary (though a higher salary would be even better). Finally, Mr. Eliot may want some security in this job, since he is now 50 and can only assume that it will be equally, if not more, difficult to get a job after Toydyno. On the other hand, he has a family to support and is concerned about having no job at all. Toydyno sounds like a good match with Mr. Eliot, if the concerns about the covenant not to compete can be addressed.

Options (pros and cons):   Mr. Eliot has three options: he can sign the contract with the terms Toydyno currently offers, he can refuse to sign the contract and walk away, or he can try to negotiate some of the terms without having Toydyno back away from its interest in him.

1. If Mr. Eliot signs the contract and accepts Toydyno's terms, he will have a job which seems to take advantage of his skill and experience (salary would have to be discussed). And it seems that unlike Kid-Vid, which is experiencing financial problems, Toydyno is going to have enormous financial success with its Knobots. On the other hand, Mr. Eliot would have to be feeling a great deal of pressure to sign the contract under the terms Toydyno currently offers. The covenant not to compete is unreasonable as to time and geography, since it prohibits an employee from selling any electronic toys to anyone anywhere. Mr. Eliot can't assume that he will be happy staying with Toydyno for the rest of his working life. When he leaves, his employment opportunities will be severely and indefinitely restricted.

2. Refusing to sign the contract and walking away is another option. There does not seems to be any advantage in doing this. Mr. Eliot would again be looking for a job. And he would not be in a worse position if he attempts to negotiate contract terms that he believes are unreasonable.

3. Mr. Eliot's best option may be to try and negotiate the terms dealing with the time and geographic restrictions. Therefore, he may want his lawyer to write a non-confrontational letter to Toydyno. The letter could express his enthusiasm for the company, his agreement to the terms relating to the computer source codes, and his understanding of the company's concerns about trade secrets. The letter would, however, express his concerns about the unlimited nature of the time and geographic restrictions. The letter could propose that Toydyno suggest a more limited restriction or propose an alternative. [See the letter to Rita Baer in Exercise 15-B(3).]

Risks: If Mr. Eliot accepts the proposed terms, he will be postponing his risk to some time in the future. At that time, he will be older and may have fewer options than he has now. If he walks away, he is faced with the risk of not finding any other employment as suitable to his interests. The risk in attempting to negotiate the terms is that Toydyno may decide he is not worth the trouble and go on to consider another candidate. On the other hand, since Mr. Eliot understands the need in principle for Toydyno to protect its trade secrets, Toydyno is less likely to refuse to deal with him further and to deny itself the opportunity to hire a salesman of talent and experience.

Letter vs. meeting: Probably a personal meeting would focus less than would a letter on the meaning of the legal terms, and more on Mr. Eliot's personal concerns. In the meeting, the lawyer would want Mr. Eliot to develop a sense of trust in the lawyer's ability to understand his concerns and to effectively represent his interests. However, it may be easier initially to explain in a letter all of the legal aspects of covenants not to compete. A lawyer might send Mr. Eliot a letter focusing on the law before the meeting, state the options generally, and say they will discuss all this and the risks when they meet in person.

Chapter Sixteen

Writing to the Court: An Introduction to Advocacy

This chapter is intended as an introduction to writing as an advocate to a court, especially writing trial and appellate briefs. The chapter includes topics that apply to persuasive writing generally. The bulk of the chapter is organized around Aristotle's three principles of persuasion: ethics, emotion, and reason, and we apply these principles to a lawyer's writing to a court. Other topics include using topic sentences as an advocate, choosing precedents, developing a theory of the case, and writing persuasively.

We think of this chapter as our answer to the question "if I had to tell the class succinctly what are the important things to think about as they change from evaluative writing to advocacy, what would I include?"

The chapter has no exercises.

Chapter Seventeen

The Trial Brief: Memorandum in Support of or in Opposition to a Motion

This is a new chapter in which we focus entirely on memoranda in support of or in opposition to a motion. We have included basic information about important (mainly pre-trial) motions and information about how the memo must respond to the requirements of the motion. Also included is a useful and generally accepted format for a memorandum of law, with information about each section and examples.

The information about writing the Argument section is fairly brief. You should refer students to the relevant sections in the next chapter where there is extensive information about writing argument.

Exercise 17-A: Answer

The first Introduction is better than the second. In the first example, the defendant has identified each count of the complaint and the grounds for its motion as to each count. The second example does not identify each of the plaintiff's claims.

Exercise 17-B: Answer

The first example is done in old fashioned language ("come now the defendants by their counsel") and legalese ("pursuant to"). The Introduction should not refer to grounds of the complaint as "inter alia." The grounds should be set out explicitly.

The second example could be considered too aggressive, but we think it is effective. This example is based on an Introduction to a memorandum written by an attorney in a major urban law firm. We might have toned it down, for example, not used both "vexatious litigation" and "blatant attempt to bully," but we don't think this goes over the line. We leave you to decide and to test it out on your class.

Exercise 17-C: Answer

1.   a. The policeman blocked the defendant's path.

     b. John lived in constant fear that his father would harm him.

     c. When only seven years old, John lost the use of his leg after the defendant (Ms. X) struck him with her automobile.

2.   a. Frank Rock will emphasize the facts that he lived with Mary Hall until the child's birth, that Mary acknowledged he was the baby's father, that he visited her and the baby in the hospital daily, that he never ceased his efforts to locate her, that he visited his daughter to the extent Mary permitted it, and that he filed a petition to establish paternity immediately after Mary and her husband made known their intent to adopt.

     b. The state agency will emphasize the facts that the baby was born out of wedlock, that Mary has a stable marital relationship, that Frank had never supported the baby and has rarely seen her, and that at the time of the petition the child was three-years old and had known only Mary and her husband as family.

Exercise 17-D: Answer

     Question Presented for Frank Rock

Whether, consistent with the Due Process Clause, the State may deny notice and an opportunity to be heard in an adoption proceeding to a biological father when the State has actual notice of his existence, whereabouts, and interest in the child.

     Question Presented for State Agency

Must the state provide a hearing to an unmarried father before it approves a nonmarital child's adoption by the child's mother and her husband when the father has never supported and rarely seen the child in the years since her birth?

Exercise 17-E: Answers

1. The Pennsylvania lower courts have recognized an exception to the employment-at-will doctrine when an employer's discharge violates a clear mandate of public policy.

2. A growing number of jurisdictions have permitted claims by children for loss of parental consortium.

3. "Post-traumatic depression" coupled with "severe depressive reaction" constitutes legal insanity and tolls the statute of limitations.

4. The municipality is liable for failing to provide police protection when the police assume a "special relationship" or "special duty" toward an individual.

Chapter Eighteen

Writing the Appellate Brief

Chapter Eighteen is a long chapter that attempts to teach students how to write each part of an appellate brief clearly and persuasively. You may want to supplement this chapter with readings in Chapter Eleven: Types of Legal Argument in Resolving Questions of Law. That chapter has useful discussions on strategic thinking and types of legal arguments that may help students to create and rebut arguments. If you are doing a statutory problem, you might also want them to reread some of Chapter Three on statutory analysis.

Most of the exercises in this chapter can be done in class. You could, if you wanted, assign different exercises to small groups and then discuss the responses at the end of class.

Exercise 18-B(2) on the Statement of the Case may be too long to do in class, unless the exercise has been read before class. You might wish to assign it as an outside assignment, dividing the class into appellants and appellees, and then discuss the responses in class. You could also ask students to outline, rather than write, their answers. They could list the relevant facts in the order they would present them and then summarize the strategy behind that order. Exercise 18-B,1 is a shorter exercise that can be done in class.

Exercise 18-C(2) requires the students to read an objective Statement of Facts and a summary of applicable law and then to write a Summary of Argument (you could also use the materials in this exercise to write a Statement of the Case). This exercise may be too complicated to do in class; you might want to assign it as homework.

Exercise 18-L is an editing exercise. If you decide to do the editing exercise in class, it might be a good idea to assign the background reading materials as homework so that class time can be spent on the actual editing exercise. At the end of class, you may wish to distribute photocopies of the sample edit which appears in this manual.

You could also use one of the memoranda you already assigned as a basis for an appellate brief exercise. Ask your students to turn the discussion of one issue into an appellate brief argument, or ask your students to write a question presented or a point heading on that issue or rewrite a thesis paragraph in argumentative style. These are good assignments to use if they can be done before the students forget too much of the memorandum.

At the end of this section of the manual, we include an explanation of topic and topic sentence outlines that your students may find helpful when rewriting drafts of their briefs.

Exercise 18-A: **Answers**

(Note: Exercise 18-C,2 also includes a question presented exercise.)

1.   Answer d is the best Question Presented. It states the legal issue clearly by referring to the statutory provisions and persuasively sets forth the legally significant facts.

     a.   This Question fails to state the cause of action and improperly uses a name.

     b.   This Question fails to supply the relevant law and facts.

     c.   This Question usurps the function of the court by assuming a favorable resolution of the legal and factual issues. It states a conclusion of law and does not include the language of the statute.

2.   Answer c is the best Question Presented. It states the cause of action clearly and sets forth the legally significant facts.

     a.   This Question usurps the function of the court by assuming a favorable resolution of the issue under scrutiny. The statement "the infant has suffered legally cognizable injuries" is a conclusion of law. The question incorrectly refers to the appellant by name.

     b.   This Question fails to supply the relevant facts and the nature of the claim.

3.   Did the District Court improperly suppress the photo identification testimony of the sole eyewitness to an armed bank robbery on the grounds that the photo identification procedure was impermissibly suggestive and the identification itself independently unreliable when all the photos exactly resembled the witness's description of the robber, the witness chose the defendant's photo with no encouragement from the

officer other than a few calming words, and the witness had seen the robber in good light and at close range for about a minute?

Exercise 18-B: **Answers**

1.   Example B is better than Example A. Although the first two paragraphs of Example A present the defendant's viewpoint fairly well, the third paragraph is weak. The author fails to include facts which support the defendant's case, such as the judge's initial reservations, the defense counsel's objections, the judge's conduct during the in camera hearing, and the equivocal nature of Sheila's responses. Example B focuses on these favorable facts.

2.   **Statement of the Case from the Appellant's Point of View**

This is an appeal by the defendant, Joan Brown, from a judgment of conviction of the crime of first degree murder rendered by the Circuit Court of Kings County.

After nine years of continual physical and psychological abuse, Joan Brown shot and killed her husband, John Brown. At trial, the defense contended that Mrs. Brown's actions were justified because she shot John in self-defense. In support of the self-defense claim, evidence of John's history of abuse and violence was introduced. Mrs. Brown testified that her husband had tormented her throughout their nine-year marriage and that this abuse had grown more frequent after the birth of their five-year-old daughter. Mrs. Brown explained that John's violence was frequently dangerous. She recounted stories in which John beat her into unconsciousness, repeatedly banged her head against a tree trunk, and broke her arm by pushing her down a flight of stairs. She testified that John had once hit her in the face with a bottle, causing gashes that required stitches.

After a particularly bad night last March, Mrs. Brown left John, taking her children, ages five and eight, to a woman's shelter. Mrs. Brown has no family in this area and had no other source of shelter. However, Mrs. Brown, who was then unemployed and had no prospect of future employment, bowed to John's request that she return home when he found her in the shelter and promised to reform.

Unfortunately, John did not keep his promise; his abusive behavior continued. Mrs. Brown said that on the morning of the fatal incident, John had threatened to "finish her off" because she had humiliated him by going to the shelter. Knowing that John always carried out his threats, Mrs. Brown took John's gun shortly before his anticipated return. She had been fearful all that day and shot John when he came through the door.

The defense attempted to support Mrs. Brown's claim of self-defense through the expert testimony of Dr. Susan Black. In deciding whether to admit this testimony, the trial court allowed both counsel to question Dr. Black without the jury present.

Dr. Black testified that she is a certified psychoanalyst who has spent many years studying the battered woman's syndrome. She explained that battered woman's syndrome is a three-stage form of family disease. During the first stage the abusive partner engages in minor physical and verbal abuse. In the second stage, there is an acute and brutal explosion of violence by the batterer. In the third stage, the battering partner expresses remorse and often promises to reform. Despite this cycle of abuse, women remain with their partners because they hope their partner will change, they fear reprisals should they attempt to leave or seek help, and they frequently lack economic resources and social support. In addition, many women are unable to leave because they are in a state of "learned helplessness." Their abusive experiences have demoralized them to such an extent that they are immobilized and feel incapable of changing their situation. Dr. Black testified that she had interviewed Mrs. Brown and had determined Mrs. Brown was subject to battered woman's syndrome. Black explained that Mrs. Brown was terrified on the day of the shooting and believed her husband's threat to "finish her off."

The defense sought to introduce Dr. Black's testimony on the grounds that it would help the jury understand why Mrs. Brown reasonably believed she was in imminent danger on the day of the shooting, and why deadly force was necessary to avoid this danger. In addition, this testimony would explain why she had not left her husband, despite his brutality. However, the trial court excluded Dr. Black's testimony on the grounds that it was not relevant to Mrs. Brown's claim of self-defense. The court stated that the objective standard used by the state of Abbott required the defendant to prove that her conduct was reasonable under the circumstances existing at the time of the offense, and Dr. Black's testimony would have no bearing on an objective evaluation of the defendant's conduct.

Joan Brown appeals her conviction on the grounds that the Circuit Court erred in excluding Dr. Black's testimony. She asks that the judgment of the Circuit Court be reversed and the case remanded for a new trial.

97

Statement of the Case from the Appellee's Point of View

On April 28, at approximately 6:30 p.m., Joan Brown shot her husband, John Brown, as he entered their home after a day at work. On the morning of the shooting, Mr. Brown had said that he was going to finish Mrs. Brown off when he got home from work because she had humiliated him when, a month earlier, she had taken the children to spend the night at a shelter for battered women. After making this statement, Mr. Brown had left for work.

Joan Brown testified that she shot her husband because he always carried out his threats and she feared for life. Thus, shortly before Mr. Brown was due back from work, about nine hours after John Brown had made his threat, Joan Brown went to their bedroom where a gun was kept and took it downstairs. There, she waited for him to come home. As Mr. Brown walked through the door, his wife raised her husband's gun and fatally shot him.

Mr. and Mrs. Brown had been married for nine years and had two children: an eight-year-old son and a five-year-old daughter. Their marriage had been marred by domestic violence, although these episodes had been separated by periods of relative calm. Mrs. Brown stated that John first became physically abusive towards her after the birth of their daughter. He had inflicted various injuries upon her, including a broken arm, an apparent concussion, and cuts requiring facial sutures.

In addition to Mrs. Brown's lengthy direct testimony, the defense also attempted to admit into evidence the expert testimony of Dr. Susan Black, a certified psychoanalyst who had examined Joan.

Dr. Black was prepared to testify that Joan Brown was subject to the battered woman's syndrome. The defense claimed that this expert testimony was relevant to Joan Brown's claim of self-defense because Dr. Black might be able to explain why Joan believed she was in imminent danger on the evening she shot her husband and why deadly force was necessary. During voir dire, the psychoanalyst described the battered woman's syndrome as a three-stage process: a tension building stage characterized by minor abuse; an acute battering stage entailing violent battering acts; and the last stage, a period of calm, contrition, and forgiveness. Dr. Black suggested that the battered woman, entrapped by this cycle, suffered from "learned helplessness" or "psychological paralysis."

The trial court excluded the testimony on the theory of battered woman's syndrome. The court concluded that Dr. Black's testimony was not relevant to the issue of self-defense, as measured by Abbott's objective standard requiring the jury to consider how an ordinary, intelligent, and prudent person would have acted under the circumstances existing at the time of the offense.

At the conclusion of the trial, the jury found Joan Brown guilty of murder, and the court sentenced her to a prison term of seven years. Joan Brown appealed her conviction to this court.

Exercise 18-C: **Answers**

1.   The sentence is weak because it doesn't identify the statute except by code citation, doesn't articulate the attorney's position on the statute's language, legislative history, or policy objectives, and doesn't phrase its arguments affirmatively (the courts are split). Moreover, you can't tell whose brief this sentence was written for. A better beginning (against fees) might look as follows.

> The overwhelming majority of the courts of appeal have denied attorney fees to an attorney who acts pro se in Freedom of Information Act (FOIA) litigation. The FOIA attorney fee provision, 5 U.S.C. § 552(a)(4)(E), applies only to parties who incur liability for fees to a third party attorney. A pro se attorney incurs no fee liability, and does not face the barriers of litigation costs that the section was intended to remove. Thus, a pro se attorney is not eligible for fees under FOIA.

2.   Appellant's Summary of Argument might look as follows:

> The trial court erred in not holding that Father Molloy was entrapped as a matter of law. Entrapment occurs as a matter of law when there is some evidence that the government agent induced the crime and the prosecution cannot prove, beyond a reasonable doubt, that the defendant was predisposed to engage in the criminal conduct.
>
> Father Malloy introduced undisputed evidence that the government agent induced Molloy to commit a crime. An inducement inquiry focuses on whether the government's conduct could have caused a person to commit a crime when that person was not predisposed to do so. Agent Smith initiated contact with Molloy, he requested Molloy's help, he offered money, and he attempted to play on the priest's sympathy. These are all indicia of inducement.

Because Molloy produced undisputed evidence of government inducement, the burden shifted to the prosecution to prove Molloy's predisposition beyond a reasonable doubt. The government produced no tangible evidence to present to the jury regarding Molloy's predisposition to commit the crime. There was no evidence of previous wrongdoing by Molloy, nor proof of ties to known terrorists. Molloy's statements regarding the plight of Catholics in Northern Ireland were unrelated to illegal weapons transportation. Since Molloy demonstrated that the government induced his criminal act, and the prosecution failed to prove predisposition beyond a reasonable doubt, the trial court should have held that he was entrapped as a matter of law.

NOTE: After your class has written the appellant's Summary, you can ask them to write the appellee's Summary.

The appellee's Summary of Argument could be written as follows:

The trial court correctly held that Father Molloy was not entrapped as a matter of law. Entrapment occurs as a matter of law when there is some proof that the government agent induced the crime and the prosecution cannot prove, beyond a reasonable doubt, that the defendant was predisposed to engage in the criminal conduct.

The government agent merely afforded Molloy an opportunity to commit the offense. Molloy was not threatened or harassed. He freely met with Agent Smith, even though Smith had previously attempted to enlist Molloy's cooperation in the crime. Smith's offer of money is also insufficient to show inducement. The defendant agreed to commit the crime as soon as Smith made an offer. As a lawyer, Molloy knew the implications. He was merely waiting until the risk was low enough and the incentive high enough.

During his third meeting with Smith, Molloy readily and willingly agreed to transport weapons illegally. His ready consent indicates that he was predisposed to commit the crime. The defendant never dismissed out-of-hand the agent's suggestions. His continued meetings with the agent point to continued interest. Moreover, his rumored association with a known terrorist, an association currently under F.B.I. investigation, also indicates predisposition. Finally, the fact that he agreed to do what he did--help in the delivery of weapons to people he knew would use them-- belies his apparently humanitarian motive of accepting the job for the sake of his charity. Thus, the trial court and the jury were correct in deciding that Molloy was not entrapped as a matter of law.

NOTE: You can also use these facts and summary of law as the basis of a Question Presented exercise, Statement of the Case exercise, or Point Heading exercise. Divide your class in half. Ask half the class to write from the appellant's point of view. The other half can write from the appellee's point of view.

Exercise 18-D: **Answer**

The headings should be in the following order (**note:** without reading carefully, the students may think they do not have enough information to put the subheadings in the correct order):

I. THE TRIAL COURT ERRED IN EXCLUDING EXPERT TESTIMONY ON THE BATTERED WIFE SYNDROME BECAUSE THAT TESTIMONY SATISFIES THE THREE-PART TEST OF RULE 230 OF THE STATE OF KENT WHICH GOVERNS THE ADMISSIBILITY OF EXPERT TESTIMONY.

    A. Dr. Platt's testimony on the Battered Wife Syndrome would aid the jury in its search for truth because the syndrome is so distinctly related to scientific and medical knowledge that it is beyond the ken of the average juror.

    B. Dr. Platt is a leading authority on the Battered Wife Syndrome and her opinions can therefore aid the trier of fact.

    C. The Battered Wife Syndrome is generally accepted in the scientific community and has been the subject of an increasing amount of research and publication.

II. THE PROBATIVE VALUE OF DR. PLATT'S TESTIMONY ON THE BATTERED WIFE SYNDROME SUBSTANTIALLY OUTWEIGHS THE DANGER OF UNFAIR PREJUDICE BECAUSE THE JURY NEEDS TO UNDERSTAND SUE GRANT'S MENTAL STATE AT THE TIME OF THE MURDER TO EVALUATE HER CLAIM OF SELF-DEFENSE.

Exercise 18-E: **Answers**

1.   Heading C is the best. Heading A does not give enough information about the claim against the defendant and the reference to the case does not help explain it. The reader does not know anything about the cases. The heading has no facts.

     Heading B also does not tell about the claim, and is a difficult sentence to understand. The sentence begins with a gerund, which is ambiguous. It's hard to tell if the word is the subject or verb. Moreover, the subject of the sentence is abstract and is separated from the verb by 15 words.

     Heading C explains the claim and connects it to the facts. Although long, the sentence is readable because it uses concrete subjects that are close to the verbs.

2.   Heading A is the best. It explains the defense and links it to the reason why the claim should fail. The sentence also has concrete subjects close to the verbs. Heading B doesn't give any explanation of the defense. Its mention of the statute it relies on is not helpful without information about the statute (and the word "only" should come after "extends").

     Heading C refers to the fact that policies are implicated here but doesn't say what they are.

     Heading D explains the defense but the sentence is difficult to understand. The subject is separated by 16 words from the verb, and the wording is poor (how can the appellant be a third person?)

3.   Heading B is the best.

     Heading A is two sentences instead of the traditional one sentence. It is repetitive ("constituted reversible error" repeats "should reverse"). The subject of the second sentence is 15 words away from the verb.

     Heading C is just a label.

     Heading B explains why the lower court committed error in a readable, although long, sentence.

4.   I. The writer uses the parties' first names. It is somewhat disrespectful to refer to an adult by first name, especially if the adult is your client, although it is more acceptable to refer to a child by first name. It is also confusing to the reader who does not know yet who Jason and Kent are. For the first reference, use full name for both, then call the father Mr. Carr, and the son Jason.

The substance of the main heading is good, although it could mention that Mr. Carr was engaged in a family purpose, and could be more concise (for example, "alleged negligent operation of a motor vehicle").

IA. This is not a good argument to the highest court of a jurisdiction. That court may agree with the lower courts, but it will do so only if it independently agrees with their reasoning. Those decisions should not be treated as binding.

IB. This heading is good in that it rests on the reasoning for parental immunity. It could be shortened, however, by taking out the explicit reference to "state policy," and just explaining the policy. For example, the middle lines could be changed to "this claim would undermine family harmony and allow tortfeasors to benefit from their own negligence."

IC. This heading combines two arguments that should be separated. The first argument (the majority of jurisdictions) again does not respect the highest court's role in making its own decisions rather than following other courts. The second argument is one of institutional competence, which is a proper argument to the supreme court, but can be more explicit. For example, "A change in the parental immunity doctrine to exclude motor vehicle accidents will undermine the state's compulsory vehicle insurance policy and should be done only by the legislature."

Exercise 18-F: Answers

1.   Example B is the better introduction. The author begins with a conclusion, concisely summarizes the constitutional issue involved and the test for determining violations, and then briefly applies that test. In example A, the author needs to connect the constitutional issue to the lower court proceedings in the problem case. The author starts with the conclusion for the opposing party. The author should have explained the Waller test before applying it. Moreover, the third prong, whether alternatives were considered, is omitted. In applying the Waller test, the author needs to make it clear that the discussion of Merta as a young victim of an assault is an effort to establish an overriding state

interest. The author should also explain that the order was sufficiently narrow because it was limited to Merta's testimony before attempting to rebut the opposing argument that a defendant has a right to his family and friends. In other words, the author's application of the <u>Waller</u> test is defensive. Finally, the author's discussion of Judiciary Law §4 belongs in a different heading.

2.   Answer:

        Possible thesis paragraph

        When Nevin threw a small bar glass at the bartender's back, he did not pose a real threat of grave or fatal injury to the bartender. Because the glass was thick and unlikely to shatter, no rational juror would conclude it was a dangerous instrument readily capable of causing death or serious physical injury, as required by P.L. 10.00, even though it did in fact cause injury. Consequently, Nevin's conviction for criminally negligent assault with a dangerous instrument should be reversed.

3.   Possible Point Heading

        THE COURT SHOULD REVERSE NEVIN'S CONVICTION FOR ASSAULT WITH A DANGEROUS INSTRUMENT BECAUSE THE SMALL AND SHATTER-PROOF DRINKING GLASS NEVIN THREW AT THE BARTENDER IS NOT AN INSTRUMENT READILY CAPABLE OF CAUSING DEATH OR OTHER SERIOUS PHYSICAL INJURY UNDER P.L. § 10.00(13).

Exercise 18-G: Answers

1.   The instant case is constitutionally indistinguishable from <u>Lee v. Weisman</u> under <u>Lee</u>'s coercion analysis. The special circumstances of the public school environment and the graduation event itself mean that the recitation of a prayer will have the same objectionable coercive effect here as in <u>Lee</u>.

2.   The passive role assigned to school officials by the Utopia policy removes the establishment problem identified in <u>Lee</u>. The <u>Lee</u> Court declined to ban prayer under all circumstances at graduation ceremonies, and would not have reached the same result without the coercion that resulted from the direct involvement of the school principal.

Exercise 18-H: Answers

1.   Example A is the better example. The writer begins with an assertion about precedents from the Supreme Court, which is the Court to which the brief was filed, and links that statement to the facts of the case. The writer then discusses the strongest precedent in detail, and provides necessary information about the holding, facts, and reasons for the decision. In example B, the writer starts with the cases from the lower courts and gives unimportant information: the remand to the trial court, the identification of the United States Court of Appeals, a fuller description of the number of pieces in the required uniform. The writer then lists a decision from another case. The discussion does not raise the reasons for the decisions.

Exercise 18-I: Answers

Suggested topic sentence for Gerald Darin:

State law may constitutionally presume the legitimacy of a child born to a married woman. A biological father's due process right to a hearing before he loses his parental rights to his nonmarital child applies only to a child born to an unmarried woman.

Suggested topic sentence for Michael Hahn:

Under the due process clause, a biological father may not be shorn of his parental rights to his child without a hearing. Supreme Court precedents have established that the due process clause protects a father who has acknowledged his child, taken responsibility for the child, and lived with the child in a family unit with the mother.

Exercise 18-J: Answers

1.   Example A marshalls the facts pretty well and relates the facts to the standards for a trial judge's reversible error where a jury requests testimony read. Example B uses the facts well but fails to relate them to the legal standard. Example C handles the facts from the prosecutor's viewpoint fairly well.

2.   Example B makes good use of the facts to argue that there is no difference between the dress requirements for male and female employees and each is required to wear a uniform. In example A, the writer concedes that the

sexes are treated differently and argues that the difference does not violate Title VII. This writer misses the opportunity to make a strong factual argument for the employer.

Exercise 18-K: **Answers**

1. The examples could be analyzed as follows:

Example 1. The author tries to minimize the weight of the <u>Carroll</u> decision by categorizing it as a deviation from a line of cases on the dress code issue. The author also suggests it is suspect because the court was divided, the case outdated, and the dissenting judge is a respected judge. These arguments are all weak arguments that carry little weight. If these techniques were used in conjunction with an argument distinguishing the problem case from the precedent's facts and reasoning, the writer would have handled the case well.

Example 2. The author minimizes <u>Carroll</u> by distinguishing the facts. On the basis of these factual distinctions, the author argues that the court's reasoning should lead to a different result in the Fields Brothers' appeal. The adverse decision is handled well, although the paragraph should begin with a more persuasive topic sentence.

Example 3. Here, the author is trying to persuade the Court that the true reasoning of those cases upon which opposing counsel relies does not support the decision for which opposing counsel contends because of factual dissimilarities. In addition, the author argues the <u>Knott</u> decision is inconsistent with the Supreme Court's prior decisions and policy. These are good arguments, but they are not presented persuasively. The writer should not begin with the opponent's position, but should instead begin with her own.

Example 4. Here, the author is trying to establish two adverse decisions as so factually dissimilar as to not warrant an extension to the problem case. The arguments here are valid, yet the paragraph should begin more affirmatively. It is difficult to tell which party wrote this argument.

Example 5.   Here, the author attempts to show that the legislative history of Title III indicates the bill was intended to control the subject matter of the problem case. How the committee witness's testimony promotes this argument is unclear, however.

2.   Example 2 could begin as follows:

Title VII does not prohibit uniforms in the workplace but requires only that a "defendant's similarly situated employees be treated in an equal manner." Carroll v. Talman Savings Ass'n, 604 F.2d 1028 (7th Cir. 1979). In Carroll, the court overturned an employer's sex-based dress code policies which required its female employees to wear a uniform but permitted male employees to wear a wide variety of attire, including sports coats and leisure suits. This dress code is easily distinguishable from the one required by Fields, where both men and women must dress in conservative business suits. Thus, Fields Brothers accomplishes the very thing that the Carroll court demands: it treats its employees equally.

3.   Instead of beginning with Fields Brothers' position, the author should begin with her own: "Although several courts have held that differences in grooming codes imposed on both sexes are permissible, grooming codes are distinguishable from dress codes imposing more severe regulations on females than on males," or "The Fields Brothers dress code regulations differ in important ways from other regulations, such as grooming codes."

4.   Example 4 could begin as follows:

Because of the special nature of ongoing domestic relationships, several courts have recognized an exception to Title III for interspousal wire tapping. Where federal courts have held a cause of action exists, the parties had already gone beyond a domestic dispute. In Jones v. Jones, the court applied Title III to a husband who had tapped a telephone at his estranged wife's separate residence, and in White v. White, the court held that there is a cause of action for a wife whose husband had hired an investigator to tap her telephone. In these cases, however, the parties were already estranged. In Jones, the parties had already separated, and the telephone was located outside of the original marital home. In White, a third party to the relationship was the agent of the intrusion. Neither of these cases involved the special nature of an ongoing domestic relationship within a marital home.

Exercise 18-L: Answer

Sample Edit

The court correctly granted Stalwart's motion to compel disclosure because CPLR § 3124 requires disclosure "if a person without having made a timely objection fails to answer interrogatories," and because CPLR § 3103 requires a protective order only to prevent "unreasonable annoyance, expense, embarrassment, disadvantage, or other prejudice." If interrogatories are necessary to a resolution, they must be answered, although they can be answered with copies of relevant documents if the answering party specifies what interrogatories are being answered.

[Then go on to apply to your facts.]

Try this

Superintendent v. Stalwart
Stalwart's Argument

parallel cite

1. Inaccurate - precedent did not address our case
2. This helps other side
3. State your conclusion

Empty - what must be looked at?

Schertzer v. Upjohn Co., 42 A.D.2d 790 (2d/ 1973) states that the Superintendent can furnish copies of relevant documents, rather than providing written answers to interrogatories. However, we must look further to determine whether the Superintendent has indeed complied with Schertzer. Schertzer sets forth requirements as to how the documents must be produced. In our case, the Superintendent failed to identify which interrogatory each document purported to answer.

Therefore, he <u>obviously</u> did not comply with Schertzer, which

requires him to a) specify which interrogatories are being

answered by production of documents and b) identify each

document to show to which particular interrogatory it related.

<u>Supra</u>. This is also supported by <u>Harlem River</u>.

Although the Superintendent's answers are definitely

inadequate, a motion to strike interrogatories may be granted if

they are "unduly prolix, vexatious and unreasonably oppressive."

See <u>Blair</u>, (59 AD 932), in which the interrogatories consists of

49 pages. However, such a motion is clearly not justified in the

case at bar, and is a blatant attempt by the Superintendent to

avoid compliance with the requirements of the CPLR.

Defendant's interrogatories, although 30 pages long and

consisting of more than 100 questions, can be easily distinguished from the set of interrogatories referred to in <u>Blair</u>. Plaintiff's

complaint is 26 pages long and charges Martin Met with

numerous types of misconduct, including conversion of corporate

assets, fraud, and breach of fiduciary duty. Plaintiff seeks

$2,684,935 in damages. The interrogatories do no more than

track plaintiff's complaint. Defendant is Executor of the Estate

of Martin Met. He is therefore a defendent in this case only by

virtue of his fiduciary capacity. He has no personal knowledge of

the allegations contained in the complaint. Interrogatories

seeking further information on each and every allegation in the

complaint are therefore essential to allow defendent to defend

himself in this case. ~~Compare~~ *See* Commissioner of the State Ins. Fund v. News World Communica, 74

AD 2d 765 cite (1st Dept. 1980). The Court should have no

difficulty in finding that the interrogatories are not

unduly long; and that the Superintendent's answers were

inadequate.

Editing: Outlining

One way to edit a draft of a brief is to make an outline of the draft. Topic outlines help to reveal the structure of a paper and to solve problems of organization. A topic outline is useful for quick reference. It can be used to check if topics and subtopics are in a logical order.

Topic sentence outlines are often even more helpful than topic outlines. In a topic sentence outline, the writer either sums up in one sentence what he says about each topic and subtopic or makes an outline of the first sentence of each paragraph. With a topic sentence outline, you can check the logical order of ideas. You can also find contradictions, identify digressions or undeveloped, unfocused, or intertwined discussions, and check on transitions. Topic sentence outlines force the writer to think through the material more clearly.

The following sample outlines illustrate the difference between topic outlines and topic sentence outlines.

Topic Outline

I.   Discussion of CPLR § 302(a)(1)

    A.   Application of first requirement (contract to supply services) to problem facts

    B.   Application of second requirement (derives revenue) to facts

II. Due Process Test

    A.   Foreseeability

        1.   <u>Volkswagen</u>

        2.   Application

    B.   Fair Play

        1.   Inconvenience

        2.   Choice of law

Many outlines begin with a thesis sentence summarizing the essential idea.

Topic Sentence Outline

THESIS: Plaintiff will argue that HC is subject to jurisdiction in New York pursuant to CPLR § 302(a)(1) and that this application comports with due process.

I.   CPLR § 302(a)(1) requires showing that the defendant entered into contract to supply services in the state and that the defendant derived substantial revenue from interstate commerce.

    A.   HC contracted to furnish plaintiffs with plans for how to start up its business.

    B.   HC received $15,000 for services rendered in the state of New York.

II. Due Process requires showing foreseeability and fair play.

    A.   Foreseeability requires a determination of whether defendant could reasonably anticipate being haled into court.

        1.   In <u>Volkswagen</u>, the court said jurisdiction would be appropriate because the manufacturer purposefully availed itself of a national market.

        2.   Here, HC was aware its activities would have a New York impact.

    B.   Fair play and substantial justice require there be no extreme inconvenience or problems with choice of law.

        1.   HC can better afford coming to NY than plaintiffs to Florida.

        2.   The contract did not require Florida law to be applied.

Chapter Nineteen

Oral Argument

Most schools include an oral argument as part of their required Moot Court program. For students, the oral argument may be the most dramatic (and most feared) part of the first year of law school. It is, however, an opportunity for them to learn the importance of preparation and to gain confidence in their ability to stand up on their own two feet and credibly present an argument. For a few students, it is positively fun.

We have tried to keep the technical instructions general, since we are aware that the formalities of oral argument vary from school to school. Therefore, if appropriate, you might want to distribute a set of instructions for oral argument that supplements those contained in this chapter. For example, your students may argue in teams, or you may want all of your students to begin by saying, "May it please the Court...," or you may want your students to open their argument by offering to give a statement of the facts in their case.

Our suggestions for oral argument emphasize preparation. Students should understand that they will not succeed by "winging it"; indeed, that would be irresponsible and unprofessional. Therefore, we include a number of specific suggestions on how they should go about preparing their oral argument.

In addition, we try to point out the purpose of oral argument and how an oral argument differs from a brief. Students may erroneously think that an oral argument is a spoken version of their written brief. We, therefore, try to direct them away from complex, techical arguments that rely heavily on authority, and towards more basic arguments that relate to fairness and common sense. We want students to be able to tell the judges why justice would be served by a decision in their client's favor and why such a decision would not have unfortunate implications. In addition, we want them to be able to distinguish between the major and minor arguments in their case and to focus on the major arguments.

Finally, we include a section on questions by the judges. Some students think they would be happy if they could simply give an uninterrupted speech on their client's behalf and then sit down. These students are afraid that the judges will ask them questions that they will be unable to answer (perhaps equating the oral argument with being called on in class). They do not see that a major purpose of oral argument is to provide an opportunity for the judges to ask questions, or if they do see this, they are too scared to care. They also may not realize that the most deadly experience is the oral argument at which the judges do not ask questions. For these students the best solution is careful preparation and repeated practice. If those students made a list of the ten questions they would least like to be asked and prepared answers to those questions ahead of time, they would find the oral argument a far less intimidating experience.

Appendix A

Exercises on Punctuation and Mechanics

Appendix A attempts to summarize those principles of punctuation and mechanics that we have noticed are most troublesome to students. You can assign the appendix at any time or use it as a reference. In your marginal comments on student work, you can refer students to Appendix A for a discussion of the relevant rule of punctuation. For errors in syntax, refer students to Chapter Ten.

The answers to the exercises in Appendix A begin on the next page. You may wish to photocopy and distribute them to your students.

Exercise A-1: Answers

1. S/V agreement (**every** is singular).

   Every decision concerning the children **was** made jointly.

2. S/Pro agreement.

   It is unlawful in N.Y. to confine **persons** against **their** will.

3. R-O (comma splice).

   The filing fee violates Doone's right to be heard in court; therefore, this fee requirement should be invalid.

4. Apos.

   The aerial surveillance was a concentrated search undertaken for the express purpose of observing defendant's activities.

5. S/Pro agreement.

   Olympia Department Store denied **it** had committed outrageous acts.

6. Introductory comma optional (the phrase is short).

   As a general rule, the court will refuse to enforce that part of the contract that is unconscionable.

7. Interrupting commas needed.

   The District Court, following a hearing, denied defendant's suppression motion.

8. S/V agreement.   N/Pro agreement

   A sufficient **connection** between the litigation and the forum state **exists**; therefore, the court possesses jurisdiction over the defendant, and **it** should hear the case.

9.   Series comma.

Based on aerial surveillance, the police entered the premises, seized certain evidence, and arrested the three defendants.

10.   No comma for restrictive modifier.

The requirement that interrogatories be answered by the production of the relevant documents was not met.

11.   Period inside quotation marks.

CPLR § 3124 requires disclosure "if a person, without having made timely objection, fails to answer interrogatories."

12.   R-O (fused sentence).

The superintendent's answer was insufficient, and the protective order was unjustified.

13.   S/V agreement. (When one subject is plural and one is singular, the verb agrees with the nearer.)

Neither defendants nor **plaintiff contests** the facts.

14.   Apos. (**It's** is the contraction of it is. **Its** is possessive.)

It's reasonable to take inflation into account.

15.   Ambiguous reference.

When Mr. Lattimore refused to answer Mr. Smith, **Smith** upset a salad tray.

16.   Period goes outside the parenthesis to close the sentence.

We needed to edit (given the twenty-page limitation).

17.   Add a fourth dot to the ellipsis to indicate the conclusion of the sentence.

The court said that "the actor disregarded the probability that severe distress would follow...."

18. Comma goes inside the quotation marks.

   Once we recognize that "designed for use" means "intended by the manufacturer," the court's application seems reasonable.

19. Apostrophe is misplaced or there is a pronoun agreement problem. (The pronoun **they** indicates a plural possessive is needed or else the pronoun needs to be changed to he or she.)

   The court denied the defendants' motion because they had not filed in time.

Or

   The court denied the defendant's motion because **she** had not filed in time.

20. Comma after the parenthesis.

   Given the limitation on length (twenty pages), we dropped that discussion.

21. Do not indicate omissions from the beginning of a quote.

   "There is no reason to strike burdensome interrogatories if they are "necessary to a resolution of defendant's affirmative defense."

Answer A-2: Answers

1.   N/Pro agreement. (Board is singular)

     The **Board**'s refusal to act makes **it** liable.

2.   Introductory comma needed. Sentence fragment. Use a colon to introduce enumerated points. Separate elements in a series with commas.

     When Jane Edwards sought to end the harassment, her complaints were disregarded: first by her supervisor, then by the Personnel Sub-Committee, and finally by the Board itself.

3.   Don't confuse the plural with the possessive.

     Churches are free to enter into contracts.

4.   Do not indicate omissions at the beginning of a quote. Add a fourth dot to ellipses to indicate the conclusion of the sentence.

     In addition to the three-prong test, the statute does not begin to run if the defendant " through fraud or concealment causes the plaintiff to relax his vigilance...."

5.   Interrupting commas needed. Period inside quotation marks.

     Rev. Bryant, who is sixty-five, refers to himself as "the rock'n roll preacher."

6.   Introductory comma needed.

     After careful consideration, I believe your sexual harassment claim is solid.

7.   Run-on (period or semicolon after "act"). Introductory comma needed after the "therefore."

     The Board failed to act; therefore, it will be held liable.

8.   Comma needed before the phrase tacked on to the end of the end.

     Jane Edwards threatened to complain to the Minnesota Department of

Human Rights, after which she was fired.

9.   Ambiguous reference (Who does "their" refer to?).

If the School does not include an invocation at graduation, **the students'**
right to free exercise of religion is violated.

10.   Apos.

He had a contractual agreement with Healthdrink Inc. not to discuss
Healthdrink and **its** deceptive advertising.

11.   Run-on (fused sentence).

The first amendment protects churches from state intervention in church
affairs, and the court is unlikely to order your reinstatement.

12.   Serial commas needed.

Her complaints were ignored by Bryant, by the Personnel Sub-
Committee, and then by the Board.

13.   Subject/verb agreement (chain/suggests).

The **chain** of events, described in Mr. Miller's testimony, **suggests** an act
of robbery.

Exercise A-3: Answers

1.   "First, the conduct must be extreme and outrageous."

      A.   Do not start a paragraph with a quote.

      B.   Start with a topic sentence announcing rule.

      C.   Cite to the source after a quotation.

      D.   Periods go inside quotation marks.

Revision

The first requirement for false imprisonment is that the conduct must be extreme and outrageous. Davis.

W. W.

2.   In Davis the court argued that if the tactics used by the creditors have   P.

involved the use of abusive language, repeated threats of ruination of

credit and threats to the debtor's employer to endanger his job, recovery

could be sustained, citing authorities and previous cases in other

m.m. jurisdictions. Id. at p. 407.

      A.   Need introductory comma after Davis.

      B.   Wrong word - courts do not argue.

      C.   Apostrophe error - **tactics** is plural, not possessive.

      D.   Put dependent clause into active voice.

      E.   Put comma before conjunction in a series.

      F.   Keep main idea of sentence in one place.

      G.   Misplaced modifier.

      H.   Citation error.

Revision

Citing authorities in other jurisdictions, the <u>Davis</u> court said that the plaintiff could recover if the creditors used tactics that involved abusive language, repeated threats of ruination of credit, and threats to the debtor's employer to endanger his job.

3. It is clear that based *wordy* on these tests liability could be established by the various tactics used by the department store.

      A.   Eliminate wordiness.

      B.   Use active voice.

      C.   Put a comma before and after an interrupting modifier following the conjunction **that** (some writers use a comma only after the modifier).

Revision

Under these tests, the department store's tactics establish liability.

4. Disregarding, for now, the fact that Augusta *legalese* the plaintiff herein didn't *avoid contracti.* actually owe money, the employee of the credit department used abusive language such as "four-flushing bitch," sent letters with statements *length* reporting Augusta's delinquency to the credit rating bureau which, if done, would substantially hurt her credit rating and/in addition, on numerous occasions threatened to report her "refusal" to pay to her employer which might be construed by a reasonable person as a serious *wordy* impairment to her continued employment.

      A.   Break into several sentences.

      B.   Eliminate wordiness and legalese.

C.   Correct comma errors.

D.   Eliminate contraction - **didn't.**

E.   Put final modifier into active voice.

F.   Work on coherence.

Revision

Disregarding the fact that Augusta did not actually owe money, the employees of the credit department used abusive language, such as "four-flushing bitch." They sent letters threatening to report Augusta's delinquency to the credit rating bureau, which, if done, would substantially hurt her credit rating. On numerous occasions, they also threatened to report her "refusal" to pay the store to her employer, a report which could jeopardize her job.

5.   An argument that could be made by Olympia, at this juncture, is that some meaningless speech from a collection department employee would

hardly be considered oppressive or outrageous.

A.   Put into active voice.

B.   Eliminate vague diction and wordiness.

Revision

Olympia could argue that some annoying speech from a collection department employee would hardly be considered oppressive or outrageous.

6.   *legalese*
One only has to look at the aforementioned decisions to see that the

wordy
store's position is weak at best.

    A.   Eliminate wordiness.

    B.   Eliminate legalese.

    C.   Use a transition word.

Revision

    Under <u>Davis</u>, however, the store's position is weak.

dangling modifier
7.   In finding only one instance of outrageous conduct in <u>Davis</u>, the number
coherence
of extreme actions here are clearly distinguishable.

    A.   Correct dangling modifier.

    B.   Clarify relation between the phrase and the clause.

Revision

Although the court found only one instance of outrageous conduct in <u>Davis</u>, a court would find a number of extreme actions here.

P/V
8.   The second factor involves the foreseeability by the store that the severe

imprecise
emotional distress will occur.

    A.   Use precise language.

    B.   Put into active voice.

    C.   This is a new issue. Begin a new paragraph.

Revision

    The second element requires Olympia to have been reasonably able to foresee that its harassment would result in the plaintiff's emotional distress.

9. "Liability extends to situations in which there is a high degree of

probability that the severe distress will follow and the actor goes ahead

restructure
in conscious disregard of it" is a direct extraction from the courts opinion.

Davis, supra.

     A.   Avoid complex subjects (the entire quote is the subject of
          the sentence).

     B.   Use apostrophe to indicate possession - **court's**.

     C.   Eliminate empty ideas.

     D.   Correct citation - supra cannot be used for cases.

Revision

In Davis, the court said that "liability extends to situations in which there is a high degree of probability that the severe distress will follow and the actor goes ahead in conscious disregard of it." Id.

                                                 R-O
10.   This standard can be used as a basis for the instant situation, thus, the
                                P/V
letter written by Augusta to the store's president is evidence that the store

                                            neither
knew of the situation in April, and the harassment was not stopped nor

correcting the billing error.

     A.   Correct run-on (comma splice).

     B.   Correct faulty parallelism.

     C.   Put into active voice.

     D.   Employ the proper correlative conjunction.

     E.   Use transition word.

Revision

Here, Augusta's letter to the store's president is evidence that the store knew of Augusta's distress in April yet it neither stopped the harassment nor corrected the billing error.

11.   If a letter to the store's president is not sufficient information, establishing foreseeability, and consequences that might result from the store's continued actions then what is?

      A.   Avoid rhetorical questions.

      B.   Correct comma error (no punctuation for a restrictive modifier).

      C.   Eliminate wordiness.

Revision

The letter to the store's president is sufficient to show the store could have foreseen that its actions would result in severe distress.

Appendix B

Answers To Bluebook Exercise

1.   <u>Johnson v. Smith</u>, 312 N.E.2d 600 (Ill. 1964).

2.   <u>Michaels v. Jordan</u>, 100 F. Supp. 5 (D.R.I. 1941).

3.   <u>Jordans v. Marsh Corp.</u>, 206 So. 2d 3 (Miss. 1959). [See R.10.2.1(c) and (h) regarding the use of business designations such as "Corp.," "Inc.," and "Bros."]

4.   <u>Marsh v. Metropolitan Hous. Inst.</u>, 6 F.3d 9 (2d Cir. 1992). [See Table 6 for words that you should abbreviate in citations. Never abbreviate the first word of a party's name.]

5.   <u>Simon v. Pauls</u>, 210 U.S. 15 (1965). [Don't give parallel cites for U.S. Supreme Court citations.]

6.   In this appeal, the defendant has raised an error he did not raise at trial. <u>See</u> <u>United States v. Carter</u>, 230 F.2d 62, 64 (__ Cir. 1971); <u>see also</u> <u>State v. Wallace</u>, 100 So. 2d 7 (Ala. 1951); <u>State v. Brown</u>, 400 P.2d 10 (Cal. 1990); <u>State v. LaFollette</u>, 312 N.W.2d 30 (Wis. 1985). [See R.1.3 and R.1.4 regarding the order of cases within string cites. List state cases in alphabetical order by state name.]

7.   In <u>Ryan v. Quinn Bros.</u>, 318 N.E.2d 6 (Mass. 1964), the court held that the defendant had violated Mass. Gen. Laws ch. 5, § 12 (___). However, the plaintiff received only nominal damages. <u>Ryan</u>, 318 N.E.2d at 10. [See Table 1. Mass. Gen. Laws is the preferred statutory code for Massachusetts.]

8.   A court may award attorney fees "reasonably <u>incurred</u>" to a successful litigant. 15 U.S.C. § 552(a)(4) (1989) (emphasis added). [Don't begin a sentence with a citation.] [Correct wording is "emphasis added."]

9.   For example, the appellee distinguishes <u>Pioneer Lands, Inc. v. Agnew</u>, 390 Md. 165, 400 A.2d 36 (1981). The Environmental Preservation Act, Md. Code Ann., [Envir.] § 36 (1992), the statute at issue in <u>Pioneer Lands</u>, is different from the one at issue here. <u>See</u> <u>Pioneer Lands</u>, 390 Md. at 165, 400 A.2d at 38. [If you give a parallel cite in the long-form

cite, you must also give a parallel cite in the short form.] [The last cite needs an introductory signal.]

10. The statute requires that three witnesses sign the will. Miss. Code Ann. § 15 (___). Only two witnesses signed the decedent's will, and the will is invalid. See Rigor v. Mortis, 182 So. 2d 10 (Miss. 1979); Macabre v. Macabre, 150 So. 2d 35 (Miss. 1972). This court has said that "[i]t is more important that the statue [sic] be enforced than the will be valid." Macabre, 150 So. 2d at 37. [See R.1.4 regarding order of cases within string cites. When citing two or more cases from the same state, list them in reverse chronological order.]

11. Gerald Gunther, Learned Hand, The Man and the Judge 37 n.148 (1994). [See R.15.]

12. Alfred W. Buckley, Videotaping Wills: A New Frontier in Estate Planning, 11 Ohio N.U. L. Rev. 271 (1984). [See R.16 and Table 13.]

———————————

———————————

Kari Aamot, a Bigelow Fellow at the University of Chicago some years ago, contributed the following idea for this exercise. "For three years now I have used your citation exercise as an in-class game, and it has worked very well. I write the "wrong" cite forms on posterboard and tape them to the board. Then the students work with their bluebooks in groups to rewrite the cites correctly. The first team to show me a perfect cite wins that round (I usually have candy prizes). The students really enjoy the game, and it seems to make them more willing to use the bluebook early on."

Drafting Writing Assignments

Writing assignments are at the heart of a legal research and writing course and can be one of our most creative teaching tools. Because of the important role they play in introducing students to legal analysis and legal writing, many teachers enjoy devising the legal problems they use for their assignments. Most also acknowledge the task to be challenging. It is no mean feat to find interesting topics of incremental complexity and to create fact patterns that force students to examine both sides of an issue.

The drafting suggestions that follow are posited on a first semester syllabus requiring three memorandum assignments and a rewrite of one memo because this seems to be the most common format for first semester legal writing courses. Nonetheless, you may want to adjust the type, number, and complexity of your assignments to suit the program at your law school. In planning your assignments, there are a number of factors to consider.

- the size of the writing class, in order to calculate a realistic turn-around time for edited assignments.

- the number of credits your course carries each semester (usually two). Most writing courses require more work than the number of credits indicates. Nonetheless, an unreasonable number of assignments may create unnecessary resentment.

- the semester calender. Try to set the deadline for the last writing assignment well before exam period begins.

- the curricular components of the course. If your course curriculum includes legal research, then you must include that instruction in your assignments. If the school requires you to provide an oral argument exercise, then you must build advocacy writing and argument into the assignments. If the school has a separate legal methods type of course, you may want to coordinate your assignments with that course. Some schools like you to coordinate your assignments with a first-year substantive course.

- the requirement of an upperclass advanced writing or research class. If your school has such a requirement, your curriculum must be planned in conjunction with those courses.

- the range of capabilities of your students.

You will also want to consider the kinds of trade-offs you are willing to make. For example,

- if you assign many rewrites or assignments that are one component of a complete document, your students will have fewer original writing and research experiences;

- if you use a variety of documents and formats, you must devote more class time to explaining the requirements of the form;

- the more difficult the topic, the more you run the risk of overwhelming some students.

One of the main points to remember is that you cannot teach everything at once within any writing assignment. Thus the writing assignments should be part of an overall course plan. Decide which basic skills you want to start with and how you want to build on them through the semester. Select topics and formats that will develop those skills incrementally, and edit your students' work with those goals in mind.

The Assignments

At the very beginning of the semester, some teachers like to give students a series of short and simple assignments which introduce students to the "building blocks" of legal analysis. For example, some people assign a case brief (see Chapter Two, Section II: "Briefing a Case"), then a comparison of cases, and then a more complete analysis (See Exercises 2-H and 3-E). Others assign one segment of a memorandum at a time.

After these short writing exercises, most teachers ask their students to write a complete memorandum. Usually, the first memorandum is a "closed" memo for which the students do not do independent research. Instead, instructors give students an assignment packet that is a closed universe. Include the problem that is the topic of the memo and the statutes and cases you want the students to use to analyze the problem. Avoid giving students secondary material, except perhaps a Restatement section. The second assignment may be a rewrite of the first memo and the third and perhaps fourth assignments may then be memoranda for which the students will do independent research. Thus you may need to begin teaching research (if that is part of the curriculum of the course) after the rewrite of the first memo and you may want to assign a library exercise. You can give your students a more complete library exercise as part of the third memo assignment.

All topics for memos should come from courses in the first-year curriculum or other areas of law that are not more difficult conceptually and that involve fairly familiar fact patterns, for example, family law. Many instructors look for topics in a variety of sources: newspapers, legal newspapers and periodicals, U.S. Law Week, A.B.A. Journal, the notes and questions of casebooks, and hornbooks for first-year classes. You can also ask colleagues for ideas about interesting issues.

Assignments One and Two: Closed Memo and Rewrite

Drafting Considerations

The topic should be a fairly simple one, either a common law problem or a simple statutory one. Use a cause of action that has a settled definition, such as a tort or a criminal statute. You can also use a cause of action for which a court clearly uses particular factors in its analysis. An assignment that involves a settled cause of acton with elements that are easy to identify will help your students to understand what is meant by issue organization. It will also enable your students to focus on applying rules to facts so they can begin to appreciate the importance of facts and how they work for and against a client's claim.

Since this memo should be short and simple, you probably should structure the facts so that only one or two elements of the cause of action are in doubt. The student should handle quickly those parts that are not in doubt and allocate more space to the elements that require some analysis. Provide facts for this issue that will make them "play" with the facts a little bit and require them to give both sides of an argument.

Depending on the sophistication of your students, include one to five authorities. Some teachers like to give out only one case for the first assignment in order to focus students on organization and simple use of a primary authority. Then they add a case or two for the rewrite to focus students on case synthesis.

Locate the problem in a real jurisdiction and include at least one case from that state so that students can learn to start with the binding precedents of the jurisdiction and to evaluate differing weights of precedents (this is one reason not to locate your case in a fictitious jurisdiction). The case should include the definition of that cause of action, but need not be factually similar to your problem. The other cases can all be from that same state or from other states (and then perhaps be more similar to the facts of your problem).

You can take liberties with the cases that you provide for this assignment. Cut out extraneous parts, rewrite difficult passages, add to a definition, etc. (If you do rewrite or add to the cases, warn the students after the assignment is completed that you have doctored the cases and they should not rely on them for any other purpose.)

The length of this assignment should depend in part on the number of authorities you include in you packet. If you include one or two cases, the memo can probably be done in three or four pages. If you include five authorities, you may want to impose a six page limit on your students.

Some teachers introduce students to case citation in the first assignment; others wait until a later assignment. If you begin teaching citation right away, make sure that you give students the information they need for citations. If you do paste up parts of pages of the cases, provide page numbers.

Goals of Assignments One and Two

The first assignment requires numerous skills. We have tried to break them down.

Analytic Skills

1.   Isolating the particular issue within the cause of action.
2.   Extracting abstract rules of law (elements, factors, tests) from cases and statutes.
3.   Recognizing and summarizing legally significant facts and reasoning in the precedent/s. Many first-year students are not accustomed to primary sources and have trouble incorporating case and statutory analysis into their papers.
4.   Analogizing and distinguishing facts. Students often do not understand the importance of facts.
5.   Identifying and evaluating opposing interpretations.
6.   Coming to a legal conclusion.

133

Writing Skills

1.   Large-scale organization

      a.   thesis paragraph - establishing a context
      b.   issue and subissue organization - separating discussions of issues and subissues
      c.   order of issues and subissues - putting issues in a logical order, i.e., threshold questions first

2.   Small-scale organization

      a.   Organization of an Issue Analysis

            i.   statement and discussion of the applicable rule
            ii.   examination of relevant case law
            iii.   application to problem case
            iv.   presentation and evaluation of opposing interpretations
            v.   conclusion

      b.   Organization of the Statement of Facts

            i.   establishing the legal context
            ii.   including significant background facts
            iii.   including legally relevant facts
            iv.   writing a clear narrative

3.   Topic and Transition Sentences
4.   Paragraph Unity and Coherence
5.   Sentence Structure: Grammar and Punctuation
6.   Tone and Diction
7.   Memo format
8.   Citation form

Research Skills

———————

      You should edit and offer comments with an eye toward the goals of the assignment. Write overall comments on the analysis and organization of the memo. In addition, you will have to line edit. First, diagnose the error in the margin. Then show the student how to correct the mistake. Be careful, however, not to rewrite every sentence, especially in the first draft. The rewrite should be the student's work, not your own. After correcting one type of mistake, save your marginal comments for diagnosis, not correction.

In the first memo, you may want to concentrate on basic analysis and organization. In the rewrite, you may want to add specific comments on case synthesis and topic sentences.

Assignments Three and Four

Drafting Considerations

The last assignments require students to do their own legal research. One way to coordinate research and writing is through a comprehensive library assignment that takes students through the research for their memo topic. Thus one requirement for the memo topic is that it provide a good library exercise. Some information should be available in most traditional research materials (including a loose-leaf service such as Law Week). The topic should have a specific key number. Topics that involve statutes that relate to a common law cause of action or that include a particular common law term are good. As a guide, this memo should be five to eight pages in length.

For a last assignment, just prepare the problem that is the topic of the memo. The students will do their own research without the aid of a prepared library assignment. If assignment three was a common law topic, this one could be a statutory one so that your students have some experience with each. The memo could be eight to ten pages.

In assignment three or four, it is nice to devise a problem that involves a threshold issue so that your students are forced not just to separate the issues but to order them logically. In one of these assignments, you might want to devise a problem that presents a question of law as well as a question of fact so that your students have the experience of writing about each. These problems should raise a couple of issues, or you could have a single main issue and several subissues.

Alternatively, if the semester is running out, you could assign students to rewrite the research memo (the third assignment) and add a short related, new issue for students to research on their own.

135

Goals of Assignment Three and Four

Analytic Skills

1.   More complex synthesizing skills

      a.   extracting legal principles from a series of cases
      b.   recognizing jurisdictional trends
      c.   construing statutes and cases that interpret the statutes

2.   More complex legal judgments

      a.   judging the quality of arguments
      b.   evaluating the weight of authority
      c.   bringing in policy arguments
      d.   supplying reasons for conclusions
      e.   balancing competing interests

Writing Skills

1.   All the skills needed in assignments one and two, with special attention to

      a.   ordering issues and subissues
      b.   organizing an issue analysis involving multiple cases
      c.   using topic sentences to introduce the idea of the paragraph

Research Skills

1.   Familiarity with basic law library research materials

      a.   Primary sources

           - statutory publications, including updating services
           - case reporters

b.   Secondary sources

        - treatises
        - encyclopedias
        - A.L.R.
        - Periodicals and their indexes

c.   Finding tools

        - digests
        - citators

d.   Computer assisted legal research

        - how to use and when to use LEXIS and WESTLAW

Commenting on Student Papers

Writing teachers often feel that commenting on student assignments is as much a struggle for them as writing those assignments is for their students. Diagnosing writing problems can be difficult. Finding clear and constructive ways to offer criticisms and suggestions can be a challenge. Nonetheless, most writing teachers feel that a good general comment sheet is a challenge worth the effort. Students seem to absorb and respond to overall comments more than marginal comments since general comments provide "the big picture" that students need in order to assess and revise their work. Moreover, providing extensive general comments early in the semester generally saves time in the long run. It is easier to provide a comprehensive critique of a short memorandum than it is to provide exhaustive analyses of long ones. If you lay an early foundation, later and more complex work will build on it. Finally, well organized general comments give structure to your conferences. If you talk through and embellish them, your discussions will be organized and purposive.

Overall Comments

We find it helpful to organize written comments around the principles of good analysis and good writing which are articulated in the text. First, we separate our comments on the different parts of the memorandum or brief. Then we organize our comments on each section by systematically examining the components of that section. This method helps us to zero in on a student's strengths and weaknesses. It also helps us to present our insights in a clear and consistent fashion.

Early in the year, our comments on each section often follow a three-part pattern. First we extract from the text some points we want our students to remember when they write that section. We also alert students to problems students commonly have in writing that section, and ways to avoid those problems. Sometimes we offer an illustration or "model" of a successful rendition of that section. At Brooklyn, we frequently put this material in a "macro" so we don't have to write it out for each student. Then we comment on the student's effort, diagnosing the problems, and offering suggestions.

In addition to being thoughtful and clearly articulated, comments should also be motivating. Students try hardest and respond to criticism best when we make them feel that a competent work product is within their grasp. Therefore, always let your students know when they have done something well and why they have done it well. ("This paragraph is good because you have compared the facts carefully.") Tell them when the next step is easily within their abilities. Even when there is little to commend, try to strike an encouraging note, especially early first semester. (You can always applaud the effort: "Your struggle with the issues in this problem is an authentic attempt to engage in legal analysis.") Always try to be positive in tone. Describe the problem in terms of what the reader needs to understand the writer's point, not in terms of the writer's failings. Say, "The reader may find a definition helpful here," not "you aren't making any sense here."

Because first-year students have to master many legal writing skills in a relatively short time, you may want to write comments which are fairly comprehensive. At the same time, it is important not to overwhelm your students. Thus, while you may decide to alert your students to a variety of concerns, it is probably a good idea to set your students particular tasks. For example, tell them to concentrate on large and small-scale organization. Once they exhibit mastery of this, focus them on writing topic and transition sentences.

Line Edits and Marginal Comments

Substantive comments in the margins are a necessary part of critiquing a paper, but they should not be used in place of a general comment sheet. Marginal notations that briefly note the problem (issues intertwined here) and that refer students to the general comment sheet (and general comments that refer to pages and paragraphs) are a good way of tying the comment sheet to the text, and *vice versa*. Asking questions in the margin is an effective way of getting students to probe deeper and of alerting students to places in the text where you had problems.

Line editing is also an important teaching tool, but only if there is a diagnosis in the margin that explains your reason for revising. Do not assume students will be able to decipher those reasons on their own. Once you've diagnosed a problem and provided a rewrite by way of illustration, stop rewriting. Diagnose the problem in the margin and let the student fix it—perhaps in conference. In marginal comments too, remember that it is important to remark on good analysis and good prose, as well as on the less positive aspects.

Sample Teacher Comments on a Student Paper

Note: The following sample comments refer to a paper on a diversity jurisdiction problem involving a minor. Keith Johnston, a ten-year-old, was injured while playing with a neighborhood friend. The incident occurred in New York, where Keith was living with his grandparents. Keith's widowed mother, Sara, was living in Massachusetts while attending business school. (She has significant contacts in both states.) She had intended to return to New York, but a Massachusetts company recently made her an offer she says she will probably accept. Sara Johnston visits Keith in New York regularly. She supports him and attends conferences at his school as well as Keith's regular medical appointments. The problem requires the students to determine whether Keith's suit, which he filed in federal court, would be likely to survive a motion to dismiss for lack of diversity jurisdiction because Keith is a resident of Massachusetts for diversity purposes.

At Brooklyn, we use a macro of the general points we want the student to remember when writing that section. The macro is in bold.

Overall Comments

You hit on the central issues here and have, therefore, a good foundation. You need to make your issue organization more apparent by beginning paragraphs with topic sentences that clearly state the rule under scrutiny and establish context. Your thesis paragraph is a pretty good introduction to the issues, although you should re-order your sentences so that the reader can more readily understand the relevance of Sara Johnston's domicile.

Question Presented

Remember, the Question Presented should not be so general that it could pertain to any case of the same type. Instead, pose the legal issue in terms of the facts that gave rise to it in your client's case. Don't use the party's names, epically when the Question Presented comes before the facts.

1) **Be careful not to beg the question by assuming the very point that needs to be decided.**
    You do a good job of avoiding this!

2) **Use the first half of the sentence to pose the legal issue; raise the facts in the second half.**

Raise some legally relevant facts. In #1, is Sara Johnston currently residing in Massachusetts? In #2, where does Keith reside? You could combine the questions.

Example: [Use full examples only when the students do not rewrite the assignment, or illustrate with an example from a different case.]

> **For purposes of a federal court's diversity jurisdiction in a suit against a New York citizen, is a minor a citizen of Massachusetts, where his mother now lives and intends to accept a job, or is he a citizen of New York, where he has spent most of his life and where he now lives with his grandparents?**

> If you decide to have two questions, you should reverse your #1 and #2. Number 2, on how to determine a minor's domicile, is the threshold question and should come first. Follow with a question on whether the mother's domicile is New York. Include the key relevant facts.

Brief Answer or Conclusion

Here you want to directly answer the QP and briefly supply your reasoning. Don't set out the rule *per se* - rather apply the rule to the facts.

> Here you need to answer the Question Presented and briefly supply your reasoning in a sentence or two (but not more if you have a conclusion at the end). In Answer #1, you give us the rule but not your conclusion about how the rule should apply.   Answer #2 is better.

Facts

The point of this section is to narrate the events that led to this dispute. A chronological organization is usually best. Include significant background facts and all legally material facts. Make sure that you have included any fact that you later use in the discussion section.

> **You might, especially if a law firm requires the facts to come first, always want to begin with a sentence that establishes the legal context so we can read the facts with an eye to the issue. Otherwise, you might want to end this way.**

141

You have most of the key facts here, but you must establish the context.

> - tell us that Keith wants to bring a suit against Kramer in federal court, but there is an issue about whether Keith could sustain a motion to dismiss a complaint for lack of diversity jurisdiction.

> - paragraph your fact statement.

Discussion

Thesis Paragraph

This paragraph introduces the problem by setting out the issues in your problem, the rules that govern those issues, and your conclusion as to how they will be applied in your case. Cite cases for the rule/s they establish, but do not raise their facts in a thesis paragraph.

Example: [Provide only when a rewrite is not required or give an example from a different case.]

Issue	**The issue is whether the court would deny the defendant's motion to dismiss for lack of diversity jurisdiction. In**
Rules	**determining jurisdiction, the plaintiff's domicile at the time of filing suit is the controlling factor. [cite] The domicile of a child of a sole surviving parent follows the domicile of that parent [cite], which is determined by that parent's intent to remain in a state for an indefinite period of time. [cite] If, however, other adults act in loco parentis and provide the child with support, maintenance, protection, and guidance,**
Application	**the child's domicile might be that of those adults. [cite] Although Keith Johnston is living with his grandparents in New York, his mother remains Keith's primary caretaker.**
Conclusion	**Her intention to remain indefinitely in Massachusetts establishes Massachusetts as Keith's domicile, and thus Keith's suit will survive the motion to dismiss.**

Your thesis paragraph has a lot of this necessary information. However, you need to establish the context of the discussion more clearly.

1)   If it is Keith's suit, why do you tell us first about Sara's residence? Give us the linking rule from <u>Ziady</u> ... that a minor acquires the domicile of his widowed mother. Then explain that a mother's domicile is determined by residence and intent (<u>Gordon</u> rule).

2)   Give us the exception to the rule, not just your conclusion (p. 3 ¶ 1)), i.e., tell us that an infant plaintiff's domicile may not be that of the widowed mother when other adults act in loco parentis and provide the child with support, maintenance, protection, and guidance. (<u>Elliot</u>) In this situation, the child's domicile might be that of the caretaker.

Then apply.

Large-scale Organization

1.   **Organize around the issues - have a separate section for each factor. Do not discuss two issues at once; do not raise an issue, drop it, and later return to it; do not organize around cases. Rather, raise cases as they illustrate the issue.**

You basically have an issue organization. However, the exception to the rule needs to be more clearly articulated. It is not clear (bottom of p. 4) why you are emphasizing Sara's contacts with Keith until later in the paragraph…when you get to <u>Elliot</u> (p.5). Thus, you might want to set out both the general rule and the exception first, then discuss the two cases, and finally explain why one would control Keith's situation.

2.   **Order issues logically. If there is a threshold issue (either a procedural issue or a substantive threshold issue), begin with it. If you have a procedural question and a substantive threshold question, begin with the procedural question and then go on to the substantive issue.**

Although you need to discuss Sara's domicile first, since you may not be able to determine Keith's domicile until you have established Sara's, you must begin by explaining the <u>Ziady</u> rule. Some of the information that comes on p. 4, paragraph 2 should precede p. 3, paragraph 2.

Small-scale Organization

For each issue, go through these steps in analysis. In the beginning, it is helpful to adhere to the order set out below since this is both a traditional order and logical.

1.   **State and then explain the applicable rule of law.**

2.   **Examine the relevant precedents [relevant facts – unless you are dealing with a question of law–reasoning, holding].**

3.   **Apply the law to fact of the instant case and compare cases -- client's arguments first.**

4.   **Present the opposing arguments [if there are valid ones].**

5.   **Evaluate and conclude.**

Issue One

1)   Work on the topic sentence setting out the first issue. 3¶2 You say the burden of proof in a diversity action rests with the plaintiff - but Sara is not the plaintiff. Moreover, the real topic seems to be on how the plaintiff can meet the burden. Connect these points, i.e., "Since a child's domicile depends on his mother's, Keith's complaint will survive a motion to dismiss for lack of diversity jurisdiction only if Sara Johnston can establish she is a citizen of Massachusetts. To do so, she must reside in Mass. and intend to remain there."

2)   Give rule before the facts.

Say -   residence + intent = domicile
    -      intent is determined by such things as driver's license, voter registration, bank accounts, real estate, etc.

Then go into <u>Gordon</u> facts and analogize
to Sara (See reordering of text pp. 3-4)

3)   New paragraph for opposing argument (4¶1).

4)   In your conclusion, you suggest Sara may not be able to show that she intended to reside in Mass. until she accepts the job. This should factor in your discussion. It should not be raised only in your conclusion.

Issue Two

1)   Give cites for rules of law.

2)   Give exception to rule after general rule (4¶2)

      a)   lay out legal grounds
              if grandparents are acting in loco parentis, then child's domicile may follow the grandparents.
      b)   lay out facts courts scrutinize - support, maintenance etc.
      c)   examine Elliot facts and Ziady facts
      d)   compare with the facts of Keith. Which case is more analogous to Keith's? Why?
      e) conclude

3)   You could handle Elliot only at the opposing argument stage (step 4) but you would still need to more carefully set out legal authority for Kramer's argument in a separate paragraph.
              Begin with the rule.
              Develop Keith facts here (support, parent conferences, etc.)

Sentence Structure
(Note: This list of pages and paragraphs lets you see at a glance what the student's major sentence level problems are).

Passive Voice	2¶2	
Wordiness	3¶2	5¶1
Comparisons	3¶2	5¶1
Fragment	5¶1	
Main Idea	3¶2	
Repeat Key Terms	3¶1	
Wrong Word	3¶2	

Grammar

R-O	Br Ans #2	5¶2
Commas	3¶1	
Reference	2¶1	4¶2
Apos	4¶2	

Memorandum

To: Professor

From: Student

Re: Motion to dismiss for lack of diversity jurisdiction in <u>Johnston v. Kramer</u>

Date: October 4, _____

QUESTION PRESENTED

Include relevant facts in #1 and #2

1.   Is Sara Johnston a resident of Massachusetts because she intends on working in this state for an indeterminative period of time after finishing school?

This is a threshold question. Put first.

2.   Is minor Keith Johnston's domicile Massachusetts, the same as that of his mother, thereby satisfying diversity jurisdiction?

BRIEF ANSWER

1.   Yes. The domicile of Sara Johnston is determined by her intent to make Massachusetts her new home for an indefinite period of time.

2.   Yes. Keith Johnston's domicile is Massachusetts because a minor's legal residence is determined by the domicile of his

R-o   surviving parent; therefore, under the present facts, diversity jurisdiction is satisfied.

STATEMENT OF FACTS

Keith Johnston is a minor presently living with his grandparents in New York. His father died three years ago. Sara

146

who is she? the mother?

, keith's mother,

Johnston lived with her parents and her son until she moved to Massachusetts to obtain an M.B.A. two years ago. She opened

clarify

there *to Massachusetts*

checking and savings accounts, changed her driver's license, and purchased a condominium ~~while~~ in Massachusetts. However, her

good

voting registration is in New York as is her car registration. She visits her son regularly, attends major parent-teacher conferences, takes Keith to regular medical appointments, and supports him financially. Last spring, Keith was injured while playing with a

clarify

, kramer, *Ref?*

neighborhood friend who is a New York resident. He subsequently moved to Massachusetts in September to live with

and then? include all relevant facts

In *he returned to his grandparents.*

his mother, ~~until~~ March of this year, Although Sara Johnston originally intended on returning to New York after finishing

what is the legal problem? Tell us

school, she has now been offered a job in Massachusetts which she says she will probably accept.

keith wants to sue Kramer in federal court if he can establish diversity jurisdiction.

DISCUSSION

A motion to dismiss for lack of diversity jurisdiction would be denied in the Southern District of New York ~~in this suit~~

P/v

Give his name in Facts.

's suit

~~by~~ Keith Johnston against the defendant Kramer. The citizenship of the plaintiff at the time of the filing of the suit is the controlling

cite

factor in determining diversity jurisdiction. A person's intent to remain in a state for an indefinite period of time acquires him

147

citizenship? domicile?

residency in that state. Gordon v. Steele, 476 F.Supp.575

Reorder ideas so we know why you raise Sara's domicile

(1974). Sara Johnston, Keith's mother, is attending school in

Massachusetts and will reside there for an indefinite period of

time, thereby making her a resident of Massachusetts. ~~Keith, a~~

This is your 1ST issue. Put after your 2nd sentence.

~~minor, is bringing suit in a federal court~~. The domicile of a minor

is the same as that of his surviving parent. Ziady v. Curley, 396

F.2nd 873 (1968). Although Keith is not presently living with his

what about Elliot?

sp

Give exception to rule.

mother, this no less diminshes the fact that she remains his

Thus? move conclusion here

primary caretaker and that his domicile is Massachusetts. ∧

Topic Sentence needed. Explain relevance of SJ discussion. State rule. Give Facts.

Since the plaintiff has the burden of proof in challenges

~~To determine whether there is diversity, where diversity~~

to claims of diversity, kJ will have to show SJ is a

~~is questioned, the burden of proof rests on the plaintiff, as in~~ *domiciliary of Mass. Domicile is determined by ___ .* *at*

Gordon v. Steele. In Gordon, a college student was found to *ww* *held*

have citizenship in the state that she attended school for the

Id. at ___ .

Gorden

ref

purposes of diversity jurisdiction. The ~~federal~~ court in ~~(this case~~

's rental of

wordy

considered ~~the fact that~~ the student's ~~had rented~~ an apartment in

determinative of her Idaho citizenship, despite

coherence keep main idea intact

Idaho, ~~and determined that~~ ∧ the possibility ~~of the student~~

that she might

cite

eventually liv~~ing~~ elsewhere or even returning to her original state. ∧

~~does not defeat the fact that her domicile is in Idaho~~. Similar to

Compare like things

student

the ~~facts~~ in Gordon, Sara Johnston attends school and owns real

property in Massachusetts. The federal court also considered the

state rules generally

subjective intent of the student of not returning to Pennsylvania relevant in determining diversity. *cite* Here, Sara Johnston intends on

accepting a job offer in Massachusetts and not returning to New

York in the foreseeable future. Therefore, it can be concluded

Do not conclude until analysis is finished

that Sara Johnston's domicile is in Massachusetts for the purposes

of diversity jurisdiction in Keith's suit. The defendant may claim,

however, that the plaintiff is still a resident of New York because

Ref *"his mother"*

she has retained her voting rights as well as her car registration in

Ref this state. In <u>Gordon</u>, the court found that this did not weigh as *continuing contacts in Pa*

heavily as the plaintiff's intent to remain in the new state for an

Id. at __.

indefinite period of time. Therefore, Sara Johnston's domicile is

Massachusetts.

This is the 1ST rule. Discuss it after the thesis paragraph. Also give exception to rule.

A minor's domicile is the same as that of his widowed

cite

mother or father. In <u>Ziady v. Curley</u>, an infant plaintiff sued a

defendant who was a citizen of North Carolina. The plaintiff was

born and raised there, but upon his parents divorce and his

father's death, the infant lived with his mother in New Jersey.

Similarly, Keith resided with his mother until she went to attend

school in Massachusetts. However, she stays in regular contact

with him, attends parent-teacher conferences and supports him

Fragment financially. ~~Thereby supporting the claim that Keith's domicile,~~

Therefore, *k's domicile*

under the <u>Ziady</u> rule, is the same as that of his mother. ~~The~~

149

Wordy ~~defendant may counter~~ that Keith's domicile is New York

However,

Topic ~~because~~ in another factually similar case, <u>Elliot v. Krear</u>, 466 F.
Sentence
on exception
If not Supp. 444 (1979), the domicile of a minor was determined to be
give
above that of his grandparents ʌwith whom the minor was actually

residing. But Keith's case is readily distinguishable from <u>Elliot</u>.

good In <u>Elliot</u>, the mother had not been exercising control as a parent

and had not been providing support. The grandparents of the

minor had been acting in loco parentis. However, unlike the

Compare *mother in Elliot*
like things ~~aforementioned case~~, Keith's mother had never relinquished her

wordy
responsibilities. Therefore, ~~it can be concluded from these facts~~

Comparisons *than to Elliot v. krear*
need 2 ~~that~~ Keith's case is more factually similar to <u>Ziady v. Curley</u>.
terms *Thus?* *conclude*

CONCLUSION

Diversity jurisdiction in this case is satisfied. Sara

Johnston's residence can be determined to be Massachusetts

because she intends to remain there for an indefinite period of

time. Keith's domicile is the same as his mother because she is his

surviving parent and because she has remained his primary

R-O
caretaker even while he remained with his grandparents. Keith

can file suit immediately following his mother's acceptance of her
What's this about? Intent not
job offer in Massachusetts. *clear enough? Discuss earlier—*
not in conclusion.

150

Student Conferences*

The Purpose of Conferences

After many years of teaching writing, we are more than ever convinced that one-on-one teaching is the best method of improving student writing. Because of this, at Brooklyn, we hold individual conferences with our students after every major writing assignment, however draining we might find these conference hours. At Northwestern, we hold one mandatory individual conference, one mandatory small group conference, and self-scheduled conferences each semester. Group conferences are briefly discussed at the end of this section.

One-on-one student conferences have two broad dimensions – a psychological and a substantive dimension. In most student conferences, we are either trying to establish rapport or we are trying to teach something, and usually we are trying to do both. As the year goes on and our students become acclimatized to law school, we can concentrate on the substantive work. Yet the mentoring relationship that develops in the conference setting is one of the most satisfying parts of a writing teacher's job.

The Psychological Dimension

The interpersonal relationship that develops during conferences is likely to increase the student's interest in writing and to create a positive attitude towards the writing course. Individual conferences convince students of our interest in them as well as in their written work. They also afford students the privacy of examining their writing without anxiety about how they appear to their peers. This combination of attention and privacy often provides students with a feeling of security which makes them increasingly responsive to criticism. Conferences also afford students the chance to ask questions about law, legal practice, legal research, the assignments, and your comments. For quiet or shy students, conferences are a safe place to take center stage and have some of their questions and concerns addressed. Finally, conferences help us to convince students of the importance of writing in the practice of law and of their ability to mature as writers.

---

*   This appendix is based on a workshop that Judith Rosenbaum and Elizabeth Fajans gave at the 1996 Conference of the Legal Writing Institute.

The Substantive Dimension

The interaction between teacher and student in the conference situation is an effective way of learning about our students' thinking processes so we can make more effective recommendations. The conference system permits us to adapt to the student's pace of learning, to review or accelerate curriculum when the student's development is out of sync with the general pace of the class, to expand on and explain our written comments, and to focus on the student's particular writing problems.

Conferences also help us to introduce students to the discourse of writing. To make meaningful evaluations of their work and meaning revisions, students must know how to talk about papers. They need a vocabulary to discuss writing. Students judge their work–but often do so in a vacuum and without clear criteria. This makes it difficult for them to revise. To become independent editors and writers, they must be able to describe the substantive and rhetorical context of their assignment to establish a *basis* for revision. Establishing criteria for evaluating work is something that goes on in both class and conference.

Any of the subjects below, as well as others, may become the content of a conference.

The Conventions of the Discipline

--What constitutes authority in law and what is its weight?

--Why do practitioners organize around issues, not cases?

--Why are writing plans like IRAC useful? When are they obstacles?

--What types of arguments do lawyers make? How are authority arguments, policy arguments, judicial administration and institutional competence arguments different? How are they weighed?

Legal Genres (legal documents)

- What kinds of document do lawyers write (office memoranda, letters, briefs, pleadings)? What are they used for? What is the purpose of each part?

- Who is the audience of these genres? What does the audience know? What does it need to know?

Substantive Content

- What actually is the law? Is authority used effectively?
- Is the analysis accurate? Thorough? Clear? Insightful?
- Are the facts argued?
- Are cases compared?
- Are there inappropriate digressions?

Logical Strategy

- What is the purpose of this document or section? To support an argument? If so, is there enough support? Is it all relevant? Is it valid? Is it appropriate? Is it specific enough? Are there alternative approaches?

Or is the document trying to persuade? Does it use positions of emphasis? Heed connotation? Frame law and facts affirmatively?

Once students can describe some of these concerns, they can think about *solutions:* Can they frame the holding broadly so case falls under it. Should they argue policy since precedents are unhelpful?

Finally, conferences can be used to practice writing and revising. You can use conference time to work with students on outlines that reflect the student's solution. Or you may decide to rewrite some transition and topic sentences with your students to give them practice in focusing and connecting their paragraphs. You can discuss paragraph coherence, which requires examining the relationship between sentences, and sentence coherence, which requires focusing on the syntactical structure of sentences, as well as the punctuation and diction of sentences. It is often helpful to have students rewrite some of their more problematic sentences before they leave your office. In this manner, conferences can be used both to discuss and to practice writing.

Institutional Constraints

Legal writing courses around the country are extremely diverse. What works in one school may be inappropriate in another since there are a number of variables that affect the length of conferences, the number of conferences you have with each student, and the content of the conferences. These variables include the following.

1) Class size and the total number of students an instructor is teaching factors in the length and number of conferences you schedule. For example, some teachers may have about 35 students in one section. Other instructors may have only 20 students in a class, but they may teach 3 sections, thus needing to find time for 60 students total.

2) The length and number of assignments tends to vary inversely with conference time. The more time teachers need to spend on grading, the less time they have, proportionately, to spend in conferences.

3) The timing of the conference may effect the length or the substance of the conference. Conferences may be longer early in the school year, when the work is unfamiliar, and shorter later. Teachers also may handle conferences differently if it is a conference to discuss a paper that has already been returned to the student, as opposed to a conference that is taking place while the student is still working on a particular assignment. A critique may be appropriate in the first case while brainstorming or a question-answer session may be appropriate in the latter situation.

The Structure of a Conference

Conferences fall into three parts: the opening, the core critique, and the closing. Early in the semester, when you are still getting to know your students and your students are still novices to the law, each part of the conference might take more time than it will take later in the semester. It is important to account for this in your scheduling.

The Opening

Take a few minutes to discuss your students' adjustment to law school. Often students have something they want to tell you - they have been out of school for 10 years, they have a new baby, they were accounting majors who never wrote. To establish rapport, you need to listen, commiserate, reassure, advise.

One good way to segue into the substantive critique is by asking the student what was hard. Some of their difficulties can be quickly resolved; sometimes you may want to delay answering. For example, if a student wasn't sure how much to say about diversity jurisdiction, you can right away discuss audience: Who are you writing for - what will they know. On the other hand, if student says "I wasn't sure how much to include in my summary of Smith," you might want to say "that's a very good question. Let's discuss it when we discuss the development of an issue analysis."

The virtue of this question/response process is that it makes the student a participant in the process–not a spectator/victim. It also ensures that student's concerns are aired.

The Critique

Your critique can be structured around the components of writing that you have been discussing in class and which are discussed in this textbook. Such a structure not only reinforces classroom lessons, but also divides the written product into parts that are visible and, therefore, more manageable.

You may want to organize your first critique differently from later ones. One effective way to proceed in a first conference is to go through a paper section-by-section, reminding students of the purpose of each section. Give examples of successful sections or pieces of them. Then look at student's work, discussing ways to revise it to meet reader's expectations, i.e., the statement of facts must, first of all, explain to the reader what happened that has created a legal problem. In so doing, it should provide all legally relevant facts, and significant background facts.

You may then wish to focus first on the paper's substance and analysis, assessing the accuracy and thoroughness of the argument, noting the successes and the mistakes and omissions, and suggesting useful avenues of pursuit. (You select and summarize authority well, but need to work on analogizing it.) Do not neglect to identify what the student did successfully. Praise not only helps students to understand your standards, but it also provides encouragement. When criticizing the work, spare your students' feelings by focusing your comments on the paper's practical effectiveness, not on the student's abilities.

After focusing on the analysis, you can look at the paper's organization, at the success of the thesis paragraph in articulating the issue and rules upon which the memo revolves, at the success of the student in ordering the issues and organizing around the issues, at the student's mastery of patterns of legal argument. Where students have trouble writing thesis paragraphs, it is often helpful to write one with the student. Where students have difficulty identifying the issues, separating the issues, or recognizing digressions, it is helpful to outline the paper to see where the organization fell apart and how it can be restructured.

Finally, leave time for practice. For a weak writer, it is often helpful to circle errors on a page or two unmarked and ask student to critique and revise these pages.

Try to make this portion of the conference a discussion, a dialogue. You might also want to try to establish at least two ways of revising so as not to "lock" your students into a grid. Students try to get you to tell them what to do. (So I should combine these sections? Use more cases?) Suggest options that leave some decision making to the student–but which gives some guidance also. Give students principles, not rules, because if you make legal writing too formulaic, your remarks will haunt you.

In second or third conferences, you may be able to omit a lot of the background discussion and zero in on a student's questions, the paper's strengths and weaknesses, and writing practice.

Closure

In closing, ask the student if anything needs clarifying, sum up key points, and prioritize. Although you may want to be comprehensive to alert students to a full range of writing concerns, (otherwise your students will say, "but you never mentioned this to me before"), it may be overwhelming to the student to address all these concerns at once. So set priorities.

Difficult Conferences

The conference is the most intense aspect of the teaching relationship. Students, particularly in the first set of conferences, are apt to react emotionally to having their work criticized. Their reaction is understandable, since the first year of law school is generally stressful to them. In addition, students are not very different from most of us–we all tend to take comments on our writing ability personally. Therefore, a teacher should be prepared for some conferences in which a student is defensive, angry, anxious, despairing, or accusing.

These conferences will require an extra degree of patience, empathy, firmness–depending on the situation. We describe below some typical scenarios you might face in conference and some common responses. It might be profitable to discuss these scenarios with your colleagues since they are likely to have other good ideas about handling these sensitive interactions.

Situation 1 – The Hostile Student

You have a ½ hour conference scheduled with Mary for 2:00, but when you look outside your office there is no one waiting. Thinking that she will be there any minute, you don't want to leave your office or get started on a new project. After 15 minutes, Mary arrives.

What do you say? How do you begin the conference?

> You would probably handle this differently depending upon whether the student's behavior was chronic or atypical. If atypical and you have time, you may agree to see her, with some warning about attorneys' busy schedules. If you don't have time, you would probably admonish her, but reschedule. If the problem is chronic, it may be appropriate to cancel the conference and to refuse to reschedule.

Mary's grade on her memo was a B. The memo has problems with large- and small-scale organization and with precision. The memo does not describe the precedents clearly and it does not explain how the precedents apply to the facts of the problem. Before you even broach these problems in conference, Mary says to you, "I was an English major in college and I have a Masters in Creative Writing. No one has ever criticized my writing or put this many marks on something I have written before."

How do you respond?

> Tell the student that a new discipline often presents new concerns, but that if his or her basic writing skills are solid, the writing will get better as the material becomes more familiar. You might also want to inform the students that even

157

experienced professionals need objective feedback and criticism–that's how we grow as writers and strengthen our work product. It is part of the legal culture to give, get, and incorporate suggestions.

Mary goes on to say, "What you are telling me to do doesn't make any sense. Look, you have this comment at the beginning that I need a 'thesis paragraph' but the information you are telling me to put here is exactly what I already wrote in the conclusion section."

What do you say now?

Talk about how the document is used. The conclusion provides a quick overview - the thesis paragraph introduces the detailed report. You probably should also address the hostility rather than ignore it. Although it is uncomfortable to discuss a student's anger at you, it is often the best way to get past it. If you say to a student, "I sense you are angry at me even though I'm really just trying to help you develop as a writer," you compel the student to examine the fairness of her attitude.

Situation 2 -- The Weeping Student

You open by asking the student, Joan, whether she has any questions about your comments. Joan says she doesn't. You ask her if she understood the comments. She nods. You say okay, she can interrupt you at any time with questions, but that meanwhile, you'll talk through the comments, focusing on how she can fill in missing steps in her reasoning so that her conclusion is more fully supported.

Tears form in Joan's eyes and roll down her cheeks. She tries, furtively, to wipe them away.

What should you do?

Ask why she is so upset. It may be your criticisms, but it may go to entire law school experience or to a personal problem. To react appropriately, you need more information.

Joan continues to cry. You suggest rescheduling the conference so Joan can collect herself. She says that given her grade, she had better stay

158

since she obviously needs the help and this is the only free time she has for the next three years.

How should you respond?

A little humor might help, "well I'm glad you're not overreacting" – and a lot of reassurance. Offer some extra help. Tell her you are willing to read and meet with her if she wants to try a rewrite. Show your confidence in her ability to improve.

Situation 3 -- The Passive Student

Jim has barely said a word all conference, although you have tried to engage him in a dialogue. You've asked him to look at the transition from issue one to issue two. "What could be a problem for the reader here," you ask. Jim says, as if guessing, "It's confusing?" "Well, yes" you say, "but why?" Jim shrugs. You suggest there is a problem with the transition. Jim say "Oh." "What does that mean to you," you ask. "I need more words," he says. "Well," you respond, "not necessarily, what you need is a sentence explaining the connection, or the change, going on here." "Oh," says Jim, "I see."

Does the student "see"? How can you check?

Get him to rewrite the transition.

Situation 4 -- The student who wants you to do his work

Your students are writing a brief. The topic involves two issues of statutory construction. The argument section may not exceed fifteen pages. Two days before the brief is due, Robert comes into your office and tells you, "I'm really getting into this topic." He adds, pulling a stack of papers out of his backpack, "I can't wait to start writing it."

1.   Should you comment on the fact he appears to be researching his topic when he should be editing and revising a final draft?

Yes. Students need to learn to manage their time effectively.

2.   He then tells you, "I just pulled these cases off the computer. I want to know what you think of them." Do you stop him here and tell him that he needs to decide that on his own? Why or why not?

> Tell him to read them first and to come back with specific questions about why he is worried about using or not using them. But make sure he makes a good faith effort before intervening. Or if your institution is opposed to this kind of feedback, explain its policy.

3.   Suppose you let him go on and he says, "I haven't actually finished reading all of them, but I think they're really good. Do you think this is a good holding?" He then starts reading and you can tell from the phrasing that he is reading a headnote setting forth the rule of law used in the case. Do you tell him that the headnote is not the holding? Why or why not?

> Fundamental mistakes should be corrected. Let's not be too miserly about sharing what we know.

4.   Robert now tells you that he has done computer research and looked in digests and ALR. He says he also found an article on this issue in the Journal of Taxation. He then asks, "Is there anywhere else that you think I should look?" Do you remind him about checking the annotated statutes? Why or why not?

> Yes...do not let students go to their own doom.

5.   He then asks you to read a small section of his paper. It could be a question presented, a case description, the thesis paragraph, or some other part. What do you do and why? Does it matter what part it is? Does it matter that he appears to be writing a first draft when you believe that he should have a second or third draft done?

> Whether you review may depend on the rules of your program. Our inclination is to review, but consistency is key.

6.   Robert then asks how many cases he should use and how many pages each section should be. The typical answer is that it all depends. What do you do when a student appears frustrated by that response?

> Outline the factors that go into case selection and length.

7.   Robert concludes this meeting by asking about the difference between an A paper and a B paper. What do you say?

> Generally an A and a B paper are competently organized and written. An A paper generally provides a more sophisticated analysis - creative but sound comparisons and rebuttals, thoughtful interpretation of rules.

Group Conferences

At Northwestern, we have been using small group conferences once each semester. After the students write the first memo, we ask a group of 4-5 students questions about how they were working, and what the hardest part of writing the memo was, etc. We also have them ask questions to us and the other students.

We have started using a different format in the second semester. We designate a subtopic from the assignment they are working on, and ask each group to act as associates in a law firm and explain to the instructor, who acts as the partner, how they analyzed this issue, how they have researched it, and what the problems are. The students must meet first as a group to prepare their presentation.

This format gives them experience working as a group and giving an informal oral presentation advising the partner, a skill they will need in practice.

Use of Collaborative Learning Techniques
to Teach Legal Writing

One of the most successful teaching devices used in the first year writing programs is collaborative learning. Collaborative learning techniques are an effective method of developing students' skills in writing and analysis. They not only significantly increase each student's active participation, but they turn classes into writing workshops. Students get increased practice in writing without increasing the amount of writing they do outside of class, and so avoid conflict with their other academic responsibilities.

Collaborative learning is based on the idea that some things are learned more effectively through small groups of students collaboratively coming to a consensus than by each of these students working individually.[2] In this setting, students are less fearful of making mistakes because they are not speaking out in front of a large class and a somewhat remote professor. Consequently, even the quietest students can overcome their inhibitions and actively participate. By participating, the students gain confidence in their abilities. Moreover, the students' progress in learning occurs not only while they work collaboratively, but carries over to their individual work as well.

Collaborative groups and peer criticism are two models of collaborative learning that can be used in writing classes that have 15-25 students, or classes that are larger.

I.   Collaborative Groups

By assigning students tasks to do in small groups during the class hour, the professor can turn the writing class into a writing workshop. The professor should begin by dividing the class into groups of approximately 5 students each, and designating one student in each group as the group's "reporter." The room must be large enough so that each of the groups can work in a different part of the room and not be distracted by any other group. Groups may or may not have fixed membership over the semester. Class time is divided into two parts. In the first part of the class, the students work in groups and are asked to reach a consensus on a task which the professor assigns. In the second part of the class, each group reports to the class as a whole, with the group's reporter presenting

---

[2] See generally Kenneth A. Bruffee, A Short Course in Writing 103-34 (2d ed. 1980).

the group's views. The professor will lead the discussion among the groups.

Be aware that the first time that a professor asks the students to work in groups, he or she is likely to be met by looks of skepticism or embarrassment. Generally this reaction disappears after the students' first experience with collaborative groups. For the first four or five minutes, the room is silent as the students read the assignment over. Even after they have finished their silent reading, many students are too shy to be the first to speak. In time, however, one or two students in each group will start talking and the professor can hear individual voices from different corners of the room. In a few minutes every student seems to be talking and individual voices are indistinct in the general buzz.

Almost every student, even those who do not volunteer to speak in any of their other classes, even a small legal writing section, will participate in the discussions of this very small group. The fear which many first year law students have about speaking out in a class of 90, or even 20, is overcome when the student is dealing informally with four other students. This does not mean, however, that the discussions are not intense. Although students can gain some reassurance from trying out their ideas in front of a non-threatening group of peers, each group has an assignment to do in class. Since each group must report to the class as a whole during the second part of the class, the students take their task very seriously. The requirement of reporting, however, is not the most important factor in motivating the students. The group itself is an extremely intense context for learning and the collaborative process generates enormous energy and effort.

The professor can give the students a wide variety of tasks to do in groups. Not all tasks will be successful. The tasks have to be limited to those that the students can successfully complete within the time available. Therefore, the task should not require too much reading because then too little group time will be available for discussion and work. (Students, however, may be given some material to look over the week before.) Nor should the students have to do too many different tasks in class, since they will likely be more productive if they can focus their efforts.

Collaborative groups can be used to teach a number of different things: to evaluate the comparative effectiveness of two thesis paragraphs, to edit poorly written sentences, to edit paragraphs for unity and coherence, to evaluate the organization of a two-page answer to a problem, to write a statement of facts, to correct errors in citation, to write questions presented and conclusions in a memorandum of law, and to construct arguments for analyzing a question of law. All of these involve the skills in writing and analysis that we wish our students to develop. Not every attempt at using collaborative learning will be successful. Nor is collaborative learning useful in all contexts. However, it is a powerful teaching mechanism because the student is the teacher. By thinking through the problem and expressing his views to his peers, the student is teaching them and teaching himself as well.

II.   Peer Criticism

Most writing teachers that we have talked to believe their own writing improved after they started teaching writing. Students, too, can learn to write more effectively by evaluating the writing of others. In the collaborative learning model of peer criticism, students evaluate (but do not grade) each other's work. Professor Kenneth Bruffee describes peer criticism as a process whereby "students learn to write helpful criticism of each other's work."[3] The operative words are learn, helpful, written, and each other's.

Students must learn how to do this kind of evaluation because it is unfamiliar and uncomfortable. They are afraid of hurting each other's feelings. They are also afraid of having friends see their work. Usually students' inhibitions about being called on in class are based more on their fear of looking foolish in front of their peers than their professors. Many believe that their professor will be understanding. But exposing their work to a fellow student requires courage, particularly if they believe, correctly or not, that the work is not very good.

In part this inhibition can be overcome by emphasizing that the criticism should be helpful. Students can benefit from learning that in legal practice, it is common for attorneys to ask other attorneys in their office to review and comment on their work. Moreover, if students are instructed to support generalizations with details and to point out strengths as well as weaknesses, they are more likely to come up with a balanced evaluation.

One exercise using peer criticism is to divide students on the same side of a Moot Court problem into pairs and to have each student edit and comment on the first draft of the brief written by the other student. A small portion of the grade for the semester may be assigned to the edit so that students will take the project seriously and so that they will feel they are getting some sort of reward

---

[3] Bruffee, *supra*, note 2, at 113.

for their work. Students should be told that although they will be helping the other student by their comments, they will, even more, be helping themselves because they will be learning how to edit their own work.

Students can be given three instructions. They must do a line edit on the brief itself, write a topic sentence outline of the Argument (see the section in the Manual on Chapter Eighteen), and conclude with a general comment sheet that discusses organization, analysis, style, and formal elements. The topic sentence outline requires the most explanation. The students should first number each paragraph in the Argument. They should then go though the entire Argument, section by section, looking at the topic sentence in each paragraph. If they think the topic sentence is a good one, they should just write it. If they think the topic sentence does not successfully state the point of the paragraph, they must re-write the topic sentence, identify the problem they saw, and explain why the change makes an improvement. In the course of doing this outline, students will become aware of organizational problems within the brief, unfocused paragraphs, and gaps in the analysis. It is a time-consuming, but very valuable assignment.

It is encouraging to read the topic sentence outlines of not only the best students, but also of the weaker students. Sometimes the weaker students gain a higher level of insight in editing another paper than they have ever been able to get in doing their own work.

III.   Pitfalls

Because collaborative learning is different from the traditional law school socratic method, students may initially be skeptical about its use. The teacher may encounter resistance in the form of rolled eyes, comments about elementary school, and refusal to get down to the task. This skepticism can be unnerving for an inexperienced teacher. Therefore, it may be wise for this teacher to put off using collaborative learning until the teacher feels confident in the classroom (but don't wait forever).

While the students are working on the assigned task, the teacher has to monitor the class to make sure that all of the groups are working on the problem. Although first year students generally do as they are directed, in a class with over 20 students, four or five groups, and a considerable amount of noise, some students may use the opportunity to chat about nonacademic issues. It may be helpful for the teacher to go from group to group and ask about their progress. It may also be helpful for a teacher who knows the skeptics to assign them as reporters for the group so they have an incentive to pay attention.

165

A related problem can occur when one group of students consistently works more quickly than the others, finishes earlier, and starts to talk about nonacademic issues. This may start distracting the other students. One way of keeping them focused is to have a secondary (and interesting) task in mind on the same materials and ask them to work on that.

Collaborative learning takes up a significant amount of class time. A teacher with an hour class may be reluctant to spend half or more of the class time with the students working in groups. Moreover, when the groups are working well, the teacher may find it difficult to maintain the level of energy when the groups stop working together and report to the class as a whole. Many teachers find themselves allocating increased time to the group work because the students are usually so involved in the task that it seems a shame to stop them. For a number of reasons, however, it is important to have the groups come together. The most important is to see what they have come up with, for students, like most of us, can support an idea as passionately when they are wrong as when they are right. The reporting of each group brings these ideas out into the open, exposing each group to the deliberations of the others. The professor can then mediate among the groups, pointing out differences of opinion and helping the larger group to come to a consensus. Certainly the professor will have a view of what the "correct" answer is. However, it is not uncommon for teachers to gain insight into a problem from the responses of their students. The group reporting also gives a student reporter practice in speaking before a group of twenty, with the confidence that at least four other people will support the student's position.

A pitfall of peer criticism is that first-year students often believe that they don't yet know enough to evaluate another student's paper. (Often, they are correct.) For first-year students, this type of assignment may be more successfully used in the second semester. For upper-year writing courses, peer evaluation assignments are usually very successful.

Notes

Notes

Notes

Notes

Notes

Notes